Special Collections in College and University Libraries

CLIP Note #35

Compiled by

Elizabeth A. Sudduth
University of South Carolina
Columbia, South Carolina

Nancy B. Newins
University of Virginia
Charlottesville, Virginia

William E. Sudduth
University of South Carolina
Columbia, South Carolina

College Library Information Packet Committee
College Libraries Section
Association of College and Research Libraries
A Division of the American Library Association
Chicago 2004

The paper used in this publication meets the minimum requirements of American National Standard for Information Sciences–Permanence of Paper for Printed Library Materials, ANSI Z39.48-1992. ∞

Library of Congress Cataloging-in-Publication Data

Special collections in college and university libraries / compiled by Elizabeth A. Sudduth, Nancy B. Newins, William E. Sudduth.
   p. cm. -- (CLIP note ; #35)
 Includes bibliographical references.
 ISBN 0-8389-8314-6 (alk. paper)
 1. Libraries--United States--Special collections. 2. Academic libraries--United States--Collection development. 3. Academic libraries--United States--Forms. 4. Library surveys--United States. I. Sudduth, Elizabeth A. II. Newins, Nancy B. III. Sudduth, William E. IV. Series: CLIP notes ; #35.

 Z688.A3U67 2005
 025.2'1877'0973--dc22
                            2004029968

Printed on recycled paper.

Printed in the United States of America.

09 08 07 06 05   5 4 3 2 1

Cover design by Jim Lange Design

TABLE OF CONTENTS

CLIPNote Committee

Brian W. Rossmann, Lead Editor
Renne Library
Montana State University
Bozeman, Montana

David A. Wright, Chair
Speed Library
Mississippi College
Clinton, Mississippi

Rick Dyson
Gray Library
Lamar University
Beaumont, Texas

David P. Jensen
Van Wylen Library
Hope College
Holland, Michigan

Liz Kocevar-Weidinger
Longwood University
Longwood University Library
Farmville, Virginia

Christopher B. Loring
William Allan Neilson Library
Smith College
Northampton, Massachusetts

William Nelson
Reese Library
Augusta State University
Augusta, Georgia

Gene Ruffin
Gwinnett University Library
Gwinnett University
Lawrenceville, GA

Marcia L. Thomas
Ames Library
Illinois Wesleyan University
Bloomington, Illinois

Ann Watson
Denison University Library
Denison University
Granville, Ohio

Corey Williams Green
Albin O. Kuhn Library & Gallery
University of Maryland, Baltimore County
Baltimore, Maryland

Introduction

Purpose

The College Library Information Packet (CLIP) Notes program started in 1980. Its purpose was clearly explained by Grady P. Morein:

> The program provides college and small university libraries with state-of-the art reviews and current documentation on library practices and procedures of relevance to them. The function of the CLIP Notes program is to share information among smaller academic libraries as a means of facilitating decision making and improving performance. The basic premise underlying the program is that libraries throughout the nation are facing numerous challenges due to changing environments and that many of these libraries can benefit by knowing how similar institutions have resolved certain problems.[1]

This CLIP Note focuses on Special Collections in college and small university libraries. For the purposes of this CLIP Note, "Special Collections" was defined to include rare books, manuscripts, and archival records administered by the small to medium size libraries represented in the CLIP Notes pool. Our hope is to provide a snapshot of the state of Special Collections in college and small university libraries which will be useful to Special Collections librarians and administrators, as well as to present examples of the policies currently in place.

Background

These are challenging times in Special Collections, in general, and for college and small university libraries, in particular. Today's challenges for Special Collections include balancing the need for access and preservation against the costs of staffing, cataloging and processing, physical space, and archival storage for a variety of formats. Web technologies offer new ways of reaching users but come with significant costs. The need for policies governing these functions has never been greater.

A survey of the literature reveals a need for continued research on Special Collections in college and small university libraries, in particular case studies, articles on successful projects, and contemporary issues. Recent articles examining the challenges faced by Special Collections librarians include Elaine Doak's case study of acquisitions and collection development in a small academic library[2] and also Susan Allen's exploration of programming for undergraduates in the Oberlin Group of libraries.[3] In addition, there

---

[1] P. Grady Morein, "What is a CLIP Note?" C&RL News 46, 5 (May 1985), 226.

[2] Elaine M. Doak, "Decisions, Decisions, Decisions: A Tale of Special Collections in the Small Academic Library." Out-of-Print and Special Collections Materials: Acquisitions and Purchasing Options. New York: Haworth Press, 2002, 41-51.

[3] Susan M. Allen, "Rare Books in the College Library: Current Practices in Marrying Undergraduates and Collections" RBML 13, 2 (1999), 110-9.

is an entire body of literature that supports the need to focus Special Collections collection development in particular in smaller libraries where resources are at a premium. Noteworthy among these articles are Ron Chepesiuk's "Isn't This Special?"[4] and Mark Herring's "Archival Treasures: Blessing – or Burden in Disguise."[5] In addition, the literature includes both articles and books about specific aspects of special collections and archives practice such as collection development, acquisitions, cataloging and processing, reference, outreach, fundraising, and the development of web resources. Both the Rare Books and Manuscripts Section (RBMS) of the Association of College and Research Libraries and the Society of American Archivists (SAA) have published guidelines and policies. These guidelines cover topics including: access, ethics, security, theft, loan for exhibition, interlibrary loan, and transfer. A significant number of libraries of all sizes make their mission statements, policies, and forms available from their Special Collections web pages, along with background information about their collections, exhibits, and finding aids.

Survey Procedure

This CLIP note follows the standard CLIP Note survey procedures outlined in CLIP Notes: Guidelines for Compilers.[6] The CLIP Note Committee of ACRL's College Libraries Section approved the proposal and reviewed the questionnaire. The compilers sought and were granted permission to use some of the questions from the 1998 Association of Research Libraries Special Collections survey with the intention of collecting parallel information.[7] Charlotte Brown, a member of the Association of College and Research Libraries Rare Books and Manuscripts Division's Publications Committee also acted as a consultant in the development of the questionnaire and later served as an expert reader.

The survey was distributed in January 2003 to test the questionnaire and to gather a sample set of policies. The final version was distributed to 260 participating libraries in February 2003 and the results were compiled over the course of the 2003-2004 academic year.

---

[4] Chepesiuk, Ron, "Isn't This Special?" American Libraries 31, no. 7 (Aug. 2000) 39.
[5] Herring, Mark Y., "Archival Treasures: Blessing – or Burden in Disguise?" American Libraries 31, no. 7 (Aug. 2000) 41-3.
[6] CLIP Notes: Guidelines for Compilers. 9 May 2004
<http://www.ala.org/ala/acrl/aboutacrl/acrlsections/collegelibraries/collpubs/clipnotesguidelines.htm>
[7] Panitch, Judith. Special Collections in ARL Libraries: Results of the 1998 Survey. Washington: Association of Research Libraries, 2001.

Analysis of Survey Results

General Information

A total of 146 of the 260 questionnaires were returned for a response rate of 56%. It is interesting to note that 16 (11%) of the responding libraries chose to fill out the survey online. One-third or 48 libraries returned policy documents and forms with their survey. A total of 58 libraries referred the compilers to policy documents and forms on their web sites.

Institutional Profiles

The majority of responding libraries or 138 (74%) are private institutions, while 38 (26%) are public institutions. The responding libraries fall into four categories in terms of the size of their student population: 12 (8%) have 1000 or less FTE students, 75 (51%) have 1000-2500 FTE students, 39 (27%) have 2500-5000 students, and 20 (14%) have over 5000 FTE students. Library Collections at 76 (52%) of reporting libraries had less than 250,000 volumes. A total of 120 (82%) of reporting institutions had less than 500,000 volumes. A small group of fourteen libraries (10%) of the responding institutions had over 750,000 volumes. Library budgets excluding salaries for 70 (50%) of participating libraries averaged under $500,000. Forty three (29%) of the responding libraries had budgets between $750,000 and $1,000,000, including 31 (21%) with budgets of $1,000,000 or more.

Profiles of Special Collections and/or Archives

Surveyed institutions reported that 139 (95%) have Special Collections and/or Archives. Seventy four respondents (35 %) reported that their Special Collections had expanded significantly in the last five years. In addition, 53 (25%) responding libraries had expanded services in the last five years. Eleven (5%) had reduced services in Special Collections in the past five years. Only 15 (7%) of libraries reported that they have deaccessioned or considered deaccessioning Special Collections materials during the past five years. Of those libraries who were considering deaccessioning, 4 of the libraries had experienced growth, in which case deaccessioning may be part of a move to focus their Special Collections.

One half of the libraries responded that they had stack growth space for 0-2 years (less than two years growth space). It is amazing that 12 (8%) of the libraries reported that they had growth space for 10 years or more. Working space for staff in Special Collections was judged adequate by 72 (53%) libraries. Public space was deemed adequate by 84 (62%) of the reporting libraries. Storage of Special Collections materials varied with 56 (41%) of the libraries reporting that all of their material was housed within the Special Collections area. However, 61 libraries (45%) reported that they housed Special Collections materials elsewhere in the library and 31 (23%) reported storing Special Collections materials elsewhere on campus. The use of off-campus storage is only reported by 6 (4%) of the responding libraries.

Library renovation projects in the past ten years relating to Special Collections were undertaken by 69 (49%) of the institutions. It is interesting to note that of the libraries with less than five years stack growth (99 libraries), 71 had not engaged in building or renovation projects in the past ten years.

Special Collections governed by an entity external to the library were held in 69 (51%) of the institutions. Examples of these collections include: college or university archives and archives of religious organizations.

Collection Descriptions

Libraries reported a wide variety of materials and formats in their Special Collections including:

> books (136 libraries or 98%)
> manuscript items/collections (124 libraries or 89%)
> institutional archives (123 libraries or 88%)
> realia/historical objects (117 libraries or 84%)
> art (91 libraries or 65%)
> maps (78 libraries or 56 %)
> music including audio formats and sheet music
> > (71 libraries or 51%)

Forty-three libraries reported having materials in other formats including visual materials (16 mm films, videocassettes, dvd's , photographs, architectural drawings, blueprints), textiles and clothing, computer output, microforms, ephemera, stamps, coins, and religious artifacts.

Bookstock comprised less than 5,000 volumes in 61% of the Special Collections. In addition, collections of over 10,000 volumes are reported in only 20% of the libraries.

Many respondents chose to highlight their most noteworthy collections or materials when asked. These responses are listed in Appendix I. The list illustrates the variety and the nature of the collections held by CLIP Note participants.

Staffing of Special Collections

Respondents reported a wide variety of position titles for those supervising Special Collections including Library Director/Dean of the Library, Head of Reference Services, Head of Reader Services, Coordinator of Technical Services, Collection Development Librarian, Professor of Classics, Bibliographic Control Librarian, etc. In 45% of the cases the supervisor had a title related to Archives and/or Special Collections. However, in 13% of the cases the Library Director acted as the supervisor of Special Collections.

Few of the libraries reported having full time staff allocated for Special Collections. Fourteen or 11% of the responding libraries reported 1 or more FTE professional staff devoted to Special Collections. Almost as many libraries reported less than .5 FTE (43%) than .5 to 1 FTE (46%) serving in Special Collections. The median staffing level reported was .46 FTE for all responding libraries.

Special Collections had even less paraprofessional support. Fifteen percent of the libraries (18) reported having more than 1 FTE paraprofessional staff and 23% (40) reported less than 1 FTE. Sixty four (52%) libraries reported no paraprofessional staffing. The median of .49 FTE is skewed by the few libraries with larger staff due to enhanced resources, funded by grants. Employment of students was somewhat more common than paraprofessionals.

Eighty percent of the supervising librarians participated in a variety of professional development or continuing education opportunities at the local, regional, and national level. The range of programs included those sponsored by regional chapters of the Society of American Archivists, state library associations and regional groups, OCLC and its regional service providers, ACRL's Rare Books and Manuscripts Section, state historical societies, the Rare Book School at the University of Virginia, and the Northeast Document Conservation Center's School for Scanning. Topics covered included: archives management, disaster preparedness, displays and exhibits, EAD (Encoded Archival Description), environmental controls, grant writing, IT/web design, preservation, etc. Respondents also mentioned keeping up with the professional literature and taking courses for credit, including web-based courses.

There is a very strong relationship between collection growth and size of staff in Special Collections with less than .5 FTE professional staff. Seventy four percent of the respondents with less than .5 FTE professional staff reported no significant growth in the past five years. In addition, only 7% of the libraries that reported more than 1 FTE of professional staff reported no significant growth in the past five years. The relationship between collection growth and paraprofessional staff numbers is strong, 54% of the respondents with less than .5 FTE paraprofessional staff reported no significant growth in the past five years. Only 6% of the libraries with more than 1 FTE paraprofessional reported no significant growth in the past five years. Also, there is a strong positive relationship between collection growth and the number of FTE student employees. Fifty four percent of the libraries with less than .5 FTE student employees reported no growth. Only two libraries with more than 1 FTE student employee reported no significant growth for the past five years. However, the relationship between student employees and significant growth is not as strong as the relationship between professional and paraprofessional staffing and significant growth.

The most noticeable statistic that can be surmised from the survey is the range of funds available to Special Collection services. From a low of zero or no money (26 of 104 reporting libraries or 25%) to a staggering high of $542,000 (55.2% of the overall total for all 104 libraries) at a single institution. This half a million dollar range skewed the mean to just under $9,500 ($9,440.90) per library. Discounting the one outlier brings the per institution average down to $4270.43 which is still well above the median of $1,000. Clearly most of the surveyed libraries do Special Collections on a shoestring budget with

58 of 104 reporting institutions (55.8%) having less than $1,000 per year to spend on support. A very select group of twelve libraries (11.5%) have over $10,000 per year to support their collections.

Income

Special Collections departments reported that they derive income from a fairly standard set of sources. Forty percent received income from endowed funds or grants, 24% received income from service fees, and 10% received income from royalties or subscription services. Institutions with the highest allocations for Special Collections were twice as likely to have income from endowed funds. Only 15% of the respondents were actively engaged in fundraising for Special Collections. Friends groups can be a valuable source of fundraising. However, only 11% of the libraries reported having a Friends group for Special Collections. Having a Friends group does appear to increase the existence of income from endowed funds, royalties, and other sources including gifts, donations, and funding through another department or another institution.

Acquisitions

Ninety six percent of the responding libraries acquired materials for Special Collections via gift. Seventy two percent of the responding libraries acquired materials through informal transfer. Fifty two percent reported that they added materials to their Special Collections by purchase. Although 88% of the respondents reported having institutional archives, only 22% of the libraries reported receiving materials through a formal transfer program.

Use of the Collections

The collections of these libraries experienced a wide range of use and contact. A total of 121 libraries responded with contact data reporting 67,293 total visits/contacts for their collections during the 2001/2002 academic year. The average library had just a fraction over 556 average visits/contacts (or about 11 per week) for the year. Over half of the libraries had 100 or less contacts (less than 2 per week) for the year. Less than 25% of the responding libraries exceeded the mean visit/contact rate for all of the libraries.

Responding libraries reported a wide and variety use their collections. Users included: students (88% of respondents), faculty (84% of respondents), college employees (83% of employees), and alumni (72.5% of respondents.) Other users included visiting (72.5%) or outside researchers (61.7%). Only 27.5% reported use by high school students. Just over 25% of the respondents reported some use by media related researchers, such as photo prospectors or film-makers.

Cataloging of Special Collections Materials

The majority of responding libraries (81%) reported that special collection materials were cataloged by cataloging staff. A smaller group of libraries (22%) reported cataloging was done by their special collections staff. In some libraries, cataloging was done by both cataloging staff and special collections staff. These figures correspond closely to the 80% of the libraries that reported cataloging their rare books for the library's OPAC and contributing records to OCLC (79%). Nearly one in eight libraries (12%) reported doing no cataloging for their special collections materials.

The percentage of non-book materials cataloged for the libraries' OPAC varied from 23% for manuscript collections to 4.5% for art and realia. Other types of non-book materials such as music (15.3%), maps (13.3%), and institutional archives (11.5%) are likely under-represented in college catalogs due to lack of staff or staff expertise with these formats. On average, only one-third to one-half of these collections were represented in OCLC. For example, libraries reported only 11.5% of their institutional archives were represented in their OPAC's compared to 8.34% that were represented in OCLC.

Processing of Archival and Manuscript Collections

In 82% of the responding libraries, archival and manuscript materials were processed by professional staff. A similar number of libraries used paraprofessional staff (53%) and student employees (52%) to process collections. Final shelf preparation was most commonly done within the Special Collections area as reported by 73% of responding libraries.

Web Presence

Fifty eight percent of the libraries reported having some web presence for their Special Collections. Fifty percent of the participating libraries had their policies available on the web. Web pages included collection specific information as well as policies for access and registration, photocopying, copyright, reproduction of images, and collection development.

As expected more libraries (75%) reported having written policies. The most common policies included access and registration, photocopying, gifts, copyright, reproduction of images, acquisitions, and collection development.

Only 21% of the responding libraries reported that at least one quarter of their finding aids for their manuscript and archival collections were on the web. Fifty-six percent of the libraries reported that none of their finding aids were accessible via the web. Finding aids available on the web were most often in html format (72%), followed by text format (24%).

Only 39% of the respondents made Special Collections materials available in digital form. Of the libraries who responded that they were engaged in digitization, 79%

reported that their projects were done in-house, 21% outsourced their projects. Digitization for preservation purposes was used by 26% percent of the responding libraries.

Conservation/Preservation

Ninety seven percent of the respondents had made a commitment to using archival housings for their materials. Seventy eight percent of the respondents stored their Special Collections materials in closed stacks. Sixty eight percent of the respondents used preservation microfilming/archival photocopying for their materials. Sixty six percent of the respondents had temperature and humidity control for their area. Surprisingly, only 49% of the libraries had fire detection systems for their collections and only 31% of the libraries had fire suppression systems for their collections. Only 29% of the responding libraries had security systems and only 7% had security cameras. Forty four percent of the libraries pursued some conservation treatment, 55% performed conservation treatment in-house and 29% outsourced their conservation treatment.

Conclusion

Special Collections in CLIP Notes libraries are predominantly comprised of printed materials from the 19th and 20th centuries and college, university, and denominational archives with a few select examples of early manuscripts and early printed books. Photographs, multi-media materials in electronic formats, as well as various types of realia are less widely held. In general, these libraries have small budgets and a low level of staffing for collections; however, budget allocations and staffing are proportional to the size and use of their collections, in part given that most collections are growing by gift rather than by purchase. The availability of introductory material, access to the online catalog, and finding aids via the Web all enable users to plan their visits. While these libraries are faced with the challenges of balancing the need for access and preservation against the costs of staffing, cataloging and processing, physical space, and archival storage for a variety of formats, many smaller college libraries are meeting these challenges through staff versatility and use of new technologies.

Selected Bibliography

Allen, Susan M. "Rare Books and the College Library: Current Practices in Marrying Undergraduates to Special Collections." RBML, 13, no. 2 (1999): 110-9.

Association of Research Libraries. Special Collections in ARL Libraries. SPEC Kit 57. Washington, D.C.: Office of Management Services, 1979.

Bengtson, Jonathan B. "Reinventing the Treasure Room: The Role of Special Collections Librarianship in the 21st Century." Advances in Librarianship 25 (2001): 187-207.

Center, Clark and Donnelly Lancaster. Security in Special Collections. SPEC Kit 284. Washington, D.C.: Association of Research Libraries, Office of Leadership and Management Services, 2004.

Chepesiuk, Ron. "Isn't This Special?" American Libraries 31 no. 7 (Aug. 2000): 39.

Cox, Richard. Closing an Era: Historical Perspectives on Modern Archives and Records Management. New York: Greenwood Press, 2000.

Doak, Elaine M. "Decisions, Decisions, Decisions: A Tale of Special Collections in the Small Academic Library. " Out-of-Print and Special Collections Materials: Acquisitions and Purchasing Options. New York: Haworth Press, 2002. 41-51.

Herring, Mark Y. "Archival Treasures: Blessing –or Burden in Disguise?" American Libraries 31, no. 7 (Aug. 2000): 41-3.

Jones, Barbara, ed. Special Collections in the Twenty-First Century. Special issue of Library Trends 52, no. 1 (Summer 2003)

Maher, William J. The Management of College and University Archives. Lanham, M.D.: Scarecrow Press, 2001.

Panitch, Judith. Special Collections in ARL Libraries: Results of the 1998 Survey. Washington, D.C.: Association of Research Libraries, 2001.

RBMS Standards and Guidelines. <http://www.rbms.nd.edu/standards>.

Schina, Bessie and Garron Wells. "University Archives and Records Programs in the United States and Canada." Archival Issues 27, no.1 (2002): [35]-48.

Society of American Archivists. A Guide to Deeds of Gift. http://www.archivists.org/publications/deed_of_gift.asp

Zanish-Belcher, Tanya. "Archives and Special Collections: A Guide to Resources on the Web." College & Research Library News 64, no. 3 (Mar. 2004): 163-6.

CLIP Note **Survey Results**

QUESTIONNAIRE ON SPECIAL COLLECTIONS IN COLLEGE LIBRARIES

For the purposes of this survey, "Special Collections" is defined to include all rare and /or otherwise special materials (books, maps, artwork) and archival collections (college or university archives, collections of manuscripts, photographs, etc.) housed separately from the circulating collections. A library may have a Collection of books that is not "rare" per se but is "special" as a unit, does not circulate, and is housed separately from the circulating collection, such as a noncirculating collection of faculty and alumni publications housed in its own room. "Special Collections" does not include separate government documents, maps and media materials collections.

1. Type of institution   **Total number of responding libraries 146**
    108 (74%) a. Private
    38 (26%) b. Public

2. Number of currently enrolled full time equivalent students
    Total number of responding libraries 146
    12   (8%) a. up to 1000
    75 (51%) b. 1000 to 2500
    39 (27%) c. 2500 to 5000
    16 (11%) d. 5000 to 7500
    4   (3%) e. over 7500

3. Number of total volumes in Library
    Total number of responding libraries 146
    76   (52%) a. up to 250,000
    44   (30%) b. 250,000 to 500,000
    12   (8%) c. 500,000 to 750,000
    9   (6%) d. 750,000 to 1,000,000
    6   (4%) e. over 1,000,000

4. Library budget for FY 2000-2001, **excluding salaries**
    Total number of responding libraries 140
    35   (25%) a. up to $250,000
    35   (25%) b. $250,000 to $500,000
    25   (18%) c. $500,000 to $750,000
    13   (9%) d. $750,000 to $1,000,000
    32   (23%) e. over $1,000,000

5. Does your library have Special Collections and/or Archives?
    Total number of responding libraries 146
    139   (95%) a. yes
    7   (5%) b. no
    Please continue if your answer is **yes**. If your answer is no, you have completed the questionnaire.

6. Please check any which describe your Special Collections program:
   Total number of responding libraries 139
   74 (53%) a. Collections have expanded significantly in the past five years
   53 (38%) b. Services have expanded significantly in the past five years
   60 (43%) c. Collections have not grown significantly in the past five years
   11 (8%) d. Services have been reduced significantly in the past five years
   9 (6%) e. Collections have been deaccessioned in the past five years
   6 (4%) f. Deaccessioning of Collection(s) is being considered

7. How many years stack growth do you have for your materials:
   Total number of responses 144
   73 (51%) a. 0-2 years
   28 (19%) b. 3-5 years
   21 (15%) c. 5-7 years
   10 (7%) d. 7-10 years
   12 (8%) e. 10 or more years

8. Work space for staff in Special Collections is:
   Total number of responding libraries 137
   72 (53%) a. adequate
   65 (47%) b. inadequate
   Please explain.

   "Part of the public service area has be used to process material since there is not enough room in the technical services area."
   "The archivist is p-t. She has enough work space but not enough storage."

9. Public space (reading room, classroom, etc.) for Special Collections is:
   Total number of responding libraries 134
   84 (63%) a. adequate
   50 (37%) b. inadequate
   Please explain.

   "Our s.p. is not publicly accessible. We would like our Rare Book College [sic] to be more accessible but lack money and space for that."
   "Not enough for an institution this size."

10. Some Special Collections materials are stored
    Total number of responses 137
    61 (45%) a. elsewhere in the Library
    31 (23%) b. elsewhere on campus
    6 (4%) c. off campus
    56 (41%) d. all Special Collections materials are housed in the Special
    Collections area

11. Has your Library engaged in any building or reconstruction projects relating to Special Collections in the past 10 years?

Total number of responding libraries 139

69 (49%) a. yes
70 (51%) b. no

Please explain.
"The central library was renovated in 2000. The Special Collections Unit had to pack and move to another Claremont library for a period of 6 months."
"The college archives has 'hit the wall' and we are talking about options, incl. storage elsewhere on campus."
"A library-wide renovation project was undertaken to provide better lighting and spaciousness. This included a renovation of the Special Collections area, due to the moving of a special research library not responsible to the library. Ultimately there was no net-loss or gain to SC and the vacated space was reallocated for administrative purposes. Overall, the library's renovation resulted in a net-loss of patron seating (100 seats)."
"Minor remodeling."

12. Are materials under the governance of another entity included in Special Collections? Examples include: college or university archives, papers of the trustees, collections belonging to a religious organization affiliated with your school, and deposit collections.

Total number of responding libraries 137

69 (51%) a. yes
68 (49%) b. no
Please explain.
"College's archives"
"College archives reports to the Library Director."
"Special Collections also houses the college archives. The institution has never adopted a clearly articulated archival or records management program, though the upper-administration routinely deposits inactive records in the archive."

13. Do your Special Collections include (please check all that apply):

Total number of responses 139

136 (98%) a. books
124 (89%) b. manuscript items/collections
123 (88%) c. institutional archives
117 (84%) d. realia/historical objects
 78 (20%) e. maps
 91 (65%) f. art
 71 (51%) g. music (audio formats, sheet music, etc.)
 43 (31%) h. other, please specify

videotapes 15
photographs 12
films 9
oral history tapes 6
audiotapes 5; audiocd 1
blueprints 2
clothing 2
microforms 2
stamps 2
architectural drawings 1
bound newspapers 1
clippings 1
computer output 1
fine press ephemera 1
local history items 1
negatives 1
plans 1
recordings of college events 1
religious artifacts 1
scrapbooks 1
textiles 1

14. Number of total volumes of book stock in Special Collections?

Total number of responding libraries 138

32 (23%) a. fewer than 1,000
53 (38%) b. 1,000 to 5,000
26 (19%) c. 5,000 to 10,000
19 (14%) d. 10,000 to 25,000
 8   (6%) e. over 25,000

15.   Approximately how many linear feet of materials are in your Special Collections?
Total number of responding libraries 84

Total 217, 282.77
Ave. 2587
Range 0-27,600

16.   What percentage of your Special Collections is comprised of:
(The total of a-i should equal 100%.)

Total number of responses 125

	Responses	Percentage	Median
a. rare books	114	26.52%	25
b. periodicals	80	4.32%	5
c. manuscripts	109	15.74%	10
d. institutional archives	113	39.05%	40
e. realia/historical objects	89	3.21%	3
f. maps	65	1.78%	1
g. art	64	1.46%	1.9
h. music	56	1.92%	1.92
i. other, please specify	43	5.84%	10

"Not rare books", videos, state and local history,
alumni authors, audio, stamps, photos, pamphlets, serials,
graphic materials, local government records, blueprints, A-V,
oral history, newsprint, scrapbooks, architectural drawings,
science fiction, posters and broadsides, vertical file, regional
history

17.   Please estimate what percentage of your printed materials were published:
(The total of a-f should equal 100%.)

Total number of responses 120

	Responses	Percentage	Median
a. before 1501 (incunables)	41	.38%	1
b. 1501-1600	62	1.08%	1
c. 1601-1700	69	2.65%	3
d. 1701-1800	86	5.4%	5
e. 1801-1900	110	25.64%	25
f. 1901-present	120	64.77%	65.8

18. Please estimate the percentage of your archival and manuscripts collections dating from:
(The total of a-g should equal 100%.)

Total number of responses 115

	Responses	**Percentage**	**Median**
a. before 1501	12	.17%	1
b. 1501-1600	15	.20%	1
c. 1601-1700	19	.27%	1
d. 1701-1800	31	.92%	2
e. 1801-1900	97	16.14%	15
f. 1901-1950	106	33.95%	15
g. 1951-present	113	47.57%	35

19. Does your library have specific or noteworthy collections as part of Special Collections? If so, please list them. Please append copies of any guides, brochures, etc. (If you have lengthy guides, the bibliographic citation is sufficient.)

Total number of responding libraries 91

See Appendix.

20. How many FTE library employees work in positions defined as professional in Special Collections?

Total number of responding libraries 130

0	**34 (26%)**
<.5	**22 (17%)**
.5-1	**60 (46%)**
>1	**14 (11%)**

low 0
high 11
median .46

21. How many FTE library employees work in positions defined as paraprofessional in Special Collections?

Total number of responding libraries 122

0	**64 (52%)**
<.5	**12 (10%)**
.5-1	**28 (23%)**
>1	**18 (15%)**

low 0
high 4.8
median .49

22. How many FTE student employees work in Special Collections?

Total number of responding libraries   122

0	**50 (41%)**
<.5	**19 (16%)**
.5-1	**35 (29%)**
>1	**18 (14%)**

low	**0**
high	**10**
median .7	

23. What is the job title of the person supervising Special Collections?

Total number of responding libraries   133

Archivist/Head of Archives 34 (26%)
Library Director 17 (13%)
Archivist/Special Collections Librarian 14 (10%)
Special Collections Librarian 12 (9%)
Head of Technical Services / Head of Technical Services Systems
      Librarian 8 (6%)
Other 48 (36%)
Other: Acquisitions Assistant, Acquisitions Librarian, Bibliographic Control
Services Librarian, Cataloging/Archives Librarian (2), Circulation Manager,
Collection Development Librarian (2), Curator, Documents/Special Collections
Librarian, Head of Collection Development/Special Collections, Head of Reader
Services, Head of Reference (2), Head of Reference and Instruction, Librarians
with named positions, Social Sciences Librarian & Coordinator of Reference and
Archives, etc.

24. In addition to supervising Special Collections, what other duties does that
person have? Please include the percentage of FTE assigned to each duty.

Total number of responding libraries   110

Other duties included the primary job responsibilities of the positions listed above
and budgeting, committee work, liaison work with academic departments,
managerial duties, including the management of student employees, reference
desk hours, teaching, and web development.

25. What type of professional development / continuing education opportunities have Special Collections staff participated in during the past three years?

Total number of responding libraries 125

None 25

National Conferences
State and Regional Conferences

Programs sponsored by: NARA, NEDCC, OCLC Networks (AMIGOS, NELINET, SOLINET), ALA, ALA RBMS, etc.

Archives related programs sponsored by SAA and regional chapters

University of Virginia Rare Books School

Subjects covered: Archives management, Cataloging, Conservation, Digitization and digital asset management, Disaster Preparedness, Displays, EAD, Environmental Controls, Grant writing, IT/Web design, Preservation, etc.

Archives courses for credit

Site visits
Professional reading, use of video & audio programming

Training on campus and programming within the Library, includes retreats

26. What is your institution's annual allocation for Special Collections (purchases/acquisitions, supplies, equipment, etc.)? Responses will be kept confidential.

Total number of responding libraries   104

26 (25.0%)	**0 or none**
32 (30.8%)	**< $1,000**
26 (23%)	**$1,001-5,000**
8 (7.7%)	**$5,001-10,000**
12 (11.5%)	**over $10,000**

Range: 0-$542,000

Total $ 981,854
Mean $ 9440.90

Median $1,000

27. Does Special Collections receive income from any of the following:
Total number of responses 139
54 (21%) a. endowed funds
26 (19%) b. grants
33 (24%) c. fees for services
6 (4%) d. royalties
8 (6%) e. subscriptions or sales
26 (19%) f. other, please specify

28. Is your institution actively engaged in fundraising specifically for Special Collections?
Total number of responding libraries 138
20 (15%) a. yes
118 (85%) b. no

29. Does your Special Collections have a friends group?
Total number of responding libraries 138
15 (11%) a. yes
123 (89%) b. no

30. How are materials for your Collections acquired? Please check all that apply.
Total number of responses 138
31 (22%) a. formal records transfer plan
100 (72%) b. informal transfer
132 (96%) c. gift
72 (52%) d. purchase
7 (5%) e. other, please specify
Other: Gift is most common

Total number of responding libraries 111

31. What hours are your Special Collections open to the public during both the general session and intersession? If access is by appointment only, please indicate.
Total number of responses 143

The majority of libraries surveyed have variation of Monday-Friday day hours. Some libraries have expanded that schedule with additional hours scheduled by appointment. Others have expanded by including some evening and weekend hours. Other variations include different schedules for the academic semesters and different interim hours. Thirty five libraries Special Collections can be accessed by appointment only. In five libraries Special Collections has the same hours as the library.

32.   How many users contacted your Special Collections department(s) in the calendar
        year 2001- 2002?
        Please include users who made contact by email, mail, phone and in-person visits.

        Total number of responding libraries 117

        Need to add table

33.   What percentage of your Special Collections department(s) users were:
        (The total of a-i should equal 100%.)

Total number of responses   120

	Responses	Percentage	Median
a. students	106	27.36%	27.5
b. faculty	101	12.39 %	10
c. employees of your college or university			
	100	20.62%	18.5
d. alumni	87	10.14%	10
e. visiting researchers	94	14.77%	10
f. distance researchers	74	10.49%	10
g. high school students and teachers			
	33	1.76%	3
h. photo prospectors, film makers, and other media researchers			
	32	1.02%	2
i. other, please elaborate			
	13	1.59%	10

34.   For Special Collections materials that are cataloged, are they

        Total number of responses 136
        30 (22%) a. cataloged by Special Collections staff
        110 (81%) b. cataloged by Cataloging Dept. staff
        16 (12%) c. not cataloged

35.   What percentage of your materials are in:

        Total number of responses 119

	Mean	Median	OPAC % of resp. libraries
a. rare books	80.14	100	94.96%
b. manuscript items/collections	23.34	40	48.74%
c. institutional archives	11.46	15	43.70%
d. realia/historical objects	4.50	50	8.40%
e. maps	13.29	75	21.85%
f. art	4.63	95	6.72%
g. music (audio formats, sheet music, etc.)	15.30	60	26.89%
h. other, please specify	8.12	100	9.24%

Have list of other

			OCLC
a. rare books	78.90	99.25	94.34%
b. manuscript items/collections	16.94	20	42.45%
c. institutional archives	8.34	10	34.91%
d. realia/historical objects	1.46	10	5.66%
e. maps	11.43	50	20.75%
f. art	2.46	50	4.72%
g.music (audio formats, sheet music, etc.)	14.32	72.5	24.53%
h.other, please specify	6.33	95	8.49%

Have list of other

36. What level of employees process archival and manuscript collections for you? Please check all that apply.
   Total number of responses 129
   - **67 (52%)** a. students
   - **29 (22%)** b. interns
   - **69 (53%)** c. paraprofessional staff
   - **106 (82%)** d. professional staff
   - **25 (19%)** e. volunteers

37. Shelf preparation (including: housing/rehousing, foldering/refoldering, creation of acid free flyers or flags, barcoding, etc.) of Special Collections materials is done by
   Total number of responding libraries 132
   - **97 (73%)** a. someone in Special Collections
   - **52 (39%)** b. someone in another area

38. Do your Special Collections have a web page(s)?
   Total number of responding libraries 137
   - **79 (58%)** a. yes
   - **56 (42%)** b. no

   If yes, please give the URL or URLS. If no, please go to question 40.

39. If your Special Collections have a web page, which of your policies are accessible there:

Total number of responding libraries 65

48   a. access, registration
24   b. copyright policies
32   c. photocopies
22   d. reproduction of images (photographs, slides)
12   e. digitization of images for patrons
4   f. digitization for department use
9   g. class or group visits
17   h. gifts
20   i. collection development
11   j. acquisitions
6   k. cataloging
6   l. transfer of books from circulating collection or other collections
9   m. records transfer
8   n. interlibrary loan
12   o. security
4   p. preservation

40. Do your Special Collections have written policies on:
Please check all that apply and append copies of all policies.

Total number of responding libraries 98

69   a. access, registration
42   b. copyright policies
56   c. photocopies
38   d. reproduction of images (photographs, slides)
20   e. digitization of images for patrons
6   f. digitization for department use
9   g. class or group visits
47   h. gifts
34   i. collection development
36   j. acquisitions
19   k. cataloging
21   l. transfer of books from circulating collection or other collections
17   m. records transfer
27   n. interlibrary loan
27   o. security
22   p. preservation

41. Approximately what percentage of the finding aids for your manuscript collections and archives are available via the Web?

Total number of responding libraries 133

75 (56%) a. none
30 (23%) b. 1-25%
 3 (2%) c. 26-50 %
 6 (5%) d. 51-75%
19 (14%) e. 76-100%

42.   What format are your guides on the Web in? Please check all that apply.
                    Total number of responding responses 71

17 (24%) a. Text
51 (72%) b. HTML
 6 (9%) c. EAD
 6 (9%) d. other, please specify

43.   Do you make Special Collections materials available in digital form?
     (If no, please go to question 46.)
                    Total number of responding libraries 136

53 (39%) a. yes
83 (61%) b. no

44.   Please describe any digitization projects you have worked on. Include any
     that are in progress or in the planning stages.
                    Total number of responding libraries 59

General digitization projects include: collections of photographs, including albums, architectural photographs, photographs of campus, college catalogues, university timeline, aerial photographs, political materials, antiquarian maps, newspaper clippings, etc.

Specific projects include: Book of Hours, Currier and Ives Collection, Josiah Parker Papers, Reynolds Family Papers, civil war and anti-slavery papers, contributions to the Ohio Memory Project, Illinois Alive!, NCECHO History of Education in North Carolina, Letters of the Marquis de Lafayette, John Brown Virtual Library, and the Digital Library of Appalachia

45.   Is digitization done   (Please check all that apply.)

Total number of responses 71

56 (79%) a. in house
15 (21%) b. outsourced
If outsourced, please identify the company or companies you have used.
14 respondents listed the following library organizations or vendors:
      OCLC 3
      Ohio Historical Society 2
      Oregon Historical Society
      Access Imaging
      Alliance Library Systems
      Alphacini
      Dan's Camera City
      Northern Micrographics
      Octavo
      To be determined

46.   What measures have you taken to protect and preserve your collection:
Please check all that apply.

Total number of responses 136

  90 (66%) a. temperature and humidity control
132 (97%) b. archival storage (acid free boxes, etc.)
  92 (68%) c. preservation microfilming, archival photocopying
  35 (26%) d. digitization for preservation purposes
  60 (44%) e. conservation treatment
  66 (49%) f. fire detection
  42 (31%) g. fire suppression
  40 (29%) h. vault
  10 (7%)   i. security cameras
  39(29%) j. security system
106 (78%) k. closed stacks
    6 (4%) l. other: attendant at desk
          light:u-v abatement
          UVI light filters and UVI film covers on exhibit materials
          Library has a security system, but no separate system for Special
             Collections. Other security measures include security policies
             and staff training.
         uv filters on fluorescent lights and windows
         Locked rooms

47. If you provide conservation treatments for your special collections, are they performed:

Total number of responding libraries 71

39 (55%) a. in house
20 (29%) b. outsourced
19 (27%) c. both

If outsourced, please elaborate:
Local conservator

Please elaborate on any unique or interesting programs or projects relating to your Special Collections.

Additional comments:

Permission to publish documents (check one of the following):
_____ Permission is given to publish in a *CLIP Note* the documents submitted with this completed survey.
_____ Permission to publish in a *CLIP Note* the documents submitted with this survey requires the following statement:

POLICIES AND FORMS

MISSION STATEMENTS

Canisius College Archives Mission Statement

The Canisius College Archives was established in 1960 to collect, preserve, and make available documents pertaining to the history of Canisius College.

The purpose for maintaining an Archives Department is fourfold: to identify and preserve items related to Canisius College history, to inform and educate the primary users of our collections, to provide administrative support to members of the current Canisius work community, and to enrich scholarship by cooperating with those members of the Canisius community engaged in making historical research relevant to student learning.

The primary audience for Archives is members of the current Canisius College community. This would include present administrators, staff, faculty, and students. Alumni and interested members of the public are also welcome to make use of the collection in a secondary user capacity. Those people engaged in genealogy pursuits are welcome to use the collection as well, although support for such research is a courtesy rather than a primary service.

Materials collected are non-current items relating to the College. "Non-current" generally refers to material more than two years old, although material that is of immediate archival importance may also be covered by this definition. Such material includes items like the Board of Trustee minutes, faculty and administrator committee minutes, policy papers of the president, vice-president, deans and directors, and official college publications such as press releases, yearbooks, and newsletters. Further material to be collected may also include other items deemed to be of sufficient long term institutional historical value. Such items might include programs from drama productions, photographs of the grounds and members of the college community, and materials relating to academic programs offered by the College.

The Archives does not serve as the official records management program for the College. The Archives does not therefore collect in any official capacity the financial, legal, or operating material pertaining to student accounts, or employee work information maintained by various departments on campus as part of their daily business. What the Archives does collect is not restricted by format, and may include paper, audiovisual materials, and online electronic documents if their subject matter is deemed appropriate.

KB
12/02

■ DAVIDSON COLLEGE ARCHIVES POLICY STATEMENT

Purpose of the Archives/Mission Statement

The Archives serves the Davidson College community in the preservation and administration of institutional records and manuscript collections. The primary purpose of the Archives is to collect, preserve, maintain and make available institutional records of administrative, legal, fiscal or historical value. The Archives also serves as a repository for manuscript collections which are related to the College and the town of Davidson, or relevant to the College's curriculum.

In conjunction with the preservation of historically valuable records, the Archives administers the College's records retention program overseeing the offsite storage, reference use of inactive records, and timely destruction of outdated records.

Records Policy

1. All records that are generated by or received in the course of official college business conducted by College offices and employees are College records and the property of Davidson College. Included within the term "records" are all documentary materials regardless of media (paper, diskette, audiotape, etc.) or characteristics (printed, typed, manuscript, audio-visual or machine-readable).

2. No College records may be destroyed or otherwise disposed of without the approval of the official in charge of the originating office and the College Archivist.

3. The Archivist shall survey all records created by and in the custody of each administrative and academic department on the campus. In cooperation with each office, schedules shall be prepared for the retention and disposal of all records. Pursuant to responsibilities, the Archivist shall have the right of reasonable access to and examination of all disposable current College records, excepting the contents of restricted documents.

4. All material of enduring value, when no longer in current use in the office to which it pertains, shall be transferred to the College Archives. Selected office files should be transferred to the Archives as they have been arranged in use, since their organization reflects the functions and activities of the office that created the records.

5. In addition, the Archives shall collect and preserve published works by Davidson College faculty, staff and alumni.

Access Policy

1. The College Archives will provide information about, copies of and/or the original documents as required for the business of the college and for research in accordance with limitations or restrictions established in the retention schedules.

2. When necessary, the office of origin or its successor may withdraw on loan any records which it has deposited, with the exception of very fragile and rare items to be supplied in copy.

Reference Policy

1. In addition to preserving records, information service is a prime function of the Archives. The Archives shall take suitable measures to arrange and prepared finding aids for the records and to answer questions from any Davidson College office or employee.

2. The Archives will provide reference service to faculty, alumni, students and visiting researchers interested in the Archives and manuscript collections. The archives will also assist faculty with bibliographic instruction related to primary research activities as needed.

Location of the Archives

The Archives exists as a department of the E.H. Little Library.

▣   TRANSFER AND STORAGE PROCEDURES

Review files annually for files scheduled to be transferred or destroyed.
For files to be transferred to INACTIVE STORAGE:

- Call the College Archives (x2632) for boxes.
    1 full file drawer = 2 boxes

- Place file folders in box - grouped by destruction date
    Do not use hanging folders. They don't fit the boxes and are an expensive way to store
        records. Do put records in labeled folders.
    Keep the folders upright with labels facing forward.
    If placing more than one record group in a box, place a marker sheet between the
        folders.

- Label the outside of the box -- in PENCIL -- with:

Office or Department name
Record group title and date range
Alphabetical, numerical, or chronological range of records
Number boxes in sequence
Examples:

Biology Department
Job Search File, 1994-1995
[A-L]
Box 1 of 2

Controller
Accounts Payable, 1993
Jan - Mar 1993
Box 1 of 6

- Contents list:
    Prepare a list by individual folder title or groups for each box. The list will be used in retrieving records as needed in the future. The office should keep a copy and send the original with the materials.
    Examples:

Box List: President's Office
            General File, 1984-1994
            Box 1 A- AR
                   Admissions
                   Alumni
                   Annual Reports
                   Architects

Dean of Faculty
Correspondence, 1990-92
Box 1   A-L
Box 2   M-Z

- Physical Transfer of Materials:
    Contact the Archives (x2632) to make arrangements for pick up and delivery.

◼ REFERENCE SERVICES AND ACCESS

- To request the return of records or to get information from records:
    Call the College Archives (x2632). We will need the name of your department, the title of the records, and the folder label.

- Restricted Records:
    Any records designated as restricted by a department or office are accessible only to the appropriate staff.

MISSION STATEMENT

Moravian College and Moravian Theological Seminary Archives

The Archives shall **collect**, **preserve**, and **facilitate access** to College and Seminary records and personal manuscripts of permanent value in documenting the history of these institutions and their precursors. The Archives shall thereby support the administrative and instructional activities of the College and Seminary, as well as institutional and independent research.

(a) **Collecting** shall involve the solicitation or donation of material from trustees; presidents, vice-presidents, and other administrators; administrative offices, academic departments, and student organizations; faculty; students and alumni; and other individuals in possession of pertinent archival material. **Records** of interest to the Archives include minutes, reports, correspondence, catalogs, yearbooks, photographs, and other published and unpublished material generated by or for the College and Seminary in the execution of their mission. **Manuscripts** of interest to the Archives include correspondence, scrapbooks, notebooks, diaries, memoirs, photographs, and other published and unpublished material of a personal nature that documents the activities of the College and Seminary. The Archives **shall not collect** artifacts, other than certain forms of memorabilia generated for reunions and other events; the published and unpublished research of faculty and students, other than student theses; or material whose only connection to the College and Seminary resides in the fact that it was created or acquired by someone associated with these institutions. Only under exceptional circumstances and in consultation with appropriate administrators shall the Archives purchase material. The Archives shall retain the right to decline or subsequently **dispose of** material that lacks permanent historical value or is duplicative of other holdings.

(b) **Preserving** shall involve the maintenance of a secure and stable physical environment; the proper storage and handling of archival material; preventive conservation measures, such as preservation photocopying; and the documentation and supervision of users to ensure the long-term survival of records and manuscripts.

(c) **Facilitating access** shall involve the arrangement and description of archival material, both physically and intellectually; the creation of finding aids, databases, and other tools designed to ease the work of users and staff; the provision of a reading room; the timely handling of written or verbal inquiries from internal and external users, including administrators, faculty, students, alumni, scholars, and genealogists; outreach activities, such as classroom presentations and exhibits; and the establishment of unambiguous access policies for all material, particularly in terms of closures and permissions.

**WILLIAMS COLLEGE
ARCHIVES AND SPECIAL COLLECTIONS**

STATEMENT OF MISSION

1. To appraise, collect, organize, describe, preserve, and make available College records of permanent administrative, legal, fiscal, and historical value.

2. To provide adequate facilities for the retention, preservation, servicing, and research use of such records.

3. To serve as a research center for the study of the College's history by members of the College and the scholarly community at large.

4. To serve in a public relations capacity by promoting knowledge and understanding of the origins, programs, and goals of the College and their development.

5. To facilitate the efficient management of the recorded information produced by the College's units and offices.

ACCESS AND USE POLICIES

AMHERST COLLEGE LIBRARY
ARCHIVES & SPECIAL COLLECTIONS

Amherst College > Library > Archives & SC > Access & Use

Access & Use

Archives
& Special
Collections
Home

Holdings
& Finding
Aids

Five College
Library
Catalogs

Five College
A&SC

Amherst
College
Related
Sites

Exhibitions

E-mail Us

The Archives and Special Collections can be reached by visiting the reading room, by mail, by phone, by fax or via the Internet. Material that is open for research is available for use in the Department reading room during regular hours. Researchers are asked to register with the Department, provide positive identification and agree to abide by the established "Terms of Access and Use." Some material is stored at a remote location and must be requested 24 hours in advance. A limited number of photocopies may be made available for research use, for those researchers unable to visit Amherst, as the materials' condition, access restrictions and staffing permit. Researchers are asked to agree to abide by the "Terms of Access and Use" which will be provided to them. Material in the Archives and Special Collections is not normally available through Inter-Library Loan.

Access and Use Policy	Permission to Publish
Registration	Reproduction
Terms of Access and Restrictions	Citation
Physical Protection of Materials	Confidentiality of Research
Copyright and Other Laws	

Commonly Requested Forms

Access and Use Policy
Any collection of unique material requires special handling. The following policies and procedures are designed to provide researchers with the greatest possible access to the materials in the Amherst College Archives and Special Collections while at the same time protecting and preserving those materials for future use. TOP

Registration
Anyone who registers, provides acceptable identification, and abides by the policies and rules of the Archives and Special Collections will be permitted to use unrestricted materials in the collection. Each reader must complete a registration card on the first visit in each fiscal year. In addition, readers must show a photographic identification card to the staff member on duty and register in the registration book. TOP

Terms of Access and Restrictions
Access to materials may be restricted by condition of gift or deposit; out of regard for the rights of individuals; because of their physical condition; or for other reasons. Manuscript material is unique and irreplaceable, and no use may be made of it that might jeopardize its preservation. In certain cases, readers may be required to consult microfilm or other copies of manuscripts, rather than originals. Readers may take only pencils, note cards, paper, and other approved writing materials into the reading areas. Coats, briefcases, books, and other personal possessions must be checked at the desk and are subject to inspection upon leaving. Materials may be used only in the reading room, during regular hours, and must be returned to the desk whenever the reader leaves the room. Please notify the staff if you wish to have materials held for your use on a subsequent day. TOP

Physical Protection of Materials

The reader is responsible for safeguarding all materials made available for use. Eating, drinking, and smoking are not permitted. Only approved writing materials may be used for taking notes while using material from the collection. "Flags" or mark ers are available for indicating material to be copied. Other methods of marking must not be used. Materials may not be leaned on, written on, folded, traced, or handled in any way likely to damage them. Readers must keep papers in their folders, maintaining the order in which they are arranged and handling them as little as possible. A staff member should be notified if papers are found to be out of order. A staff member should also be shown any torn or very fragile materials that might be in need of repair. During use, folders must be kept flat on the table. Books must be used on the table, properly supported if necessary. Readers may be asked to wear special gloves when handling certain materials, such as photographs. TOP

Copyright and Other Laws

Use of manuscripts and published materials is subject to provisions of the copyright law. Laws against libel and invasion of privacy may also apply. Readers assume full responsibility for any legal questions that may arise as the result of their use of materials in the collections. TOP

Permission to Publish

Permission to examine materials, or to obtain copies, does not imply the right to publish them, in whole or in part. A separate written request for permission to publish must be made to the Archivist or to the Curator of Special Collections, as approp riate. Permission must also be obtained from the author or anyone else who holds copyright or other publication rights. TOP

Reproduction

If photocopying or other reproduction can be done without injury to the materials and does not violate copyright or other restrictions, a single copy of any item will ordinarily be made for the researcher's personal use, upon written request and payment of the appropriate fees. Such copies may not be later duplicated, nor may they be transferred to or deposited with another person or institution without written permission from the Amherst College Archives or Special Collections. For some collections, the researcher may be required to return copies after use. "Flags" or markers are available for indicating material to be copied. No other method of marking materials for copying may be used. Because staff and facilities are limited, it will not always be possible to provide copying service immediately, especially if large numbers of copies are requested. Orders will be taken for later pick-up or mail delivery. TOP

- **Reproduction and Use Fees**

Citation

The location and description of manuscript or archival materials referred to or quoted in papers (published or unpublished) should be cited accurately and completely. The following sample citations illustrate the information to be included:

> Manuscript materials: Allen Tate to Louise Bogan, 10 January 1965, in Louise Bogan Papers (Box IV, Folder 1), Archives and Special Collections, Amherst College Library.

> Archival materials: Theodore Baird, Working papers for assignment development and class meetings, 1943-1945, in English Department Records: English 1-2 (Box 1, Folder 43), Archives and Special Collections, Amherst College Library. Researchers are encouraged to provide a free copy of any publication in which Archives or Special Collections material is referred to or quoted.

Confidentiality of Research

Information about researchers' work in the Archives and Special Collections, including their topics and the materials used, will be kept strictly confidential. TOP

The Butler University Libraries
Special Collections/Rare Books/University Archives
4600 Sunset Avenue, Indianapolis, IN 46208
317-940-9265
www.butler.edu/www/library/rare

USING SPECIAL COLLECTIONS, RARE BOOKS, AND UNIVERSITY ARCHIVES

Welcome to Irwin Library and its Special Collections, Rare Books, and University Archives section. We are open to the public and provide reference and reading services. Materials do not circulate; researchers must use them in the reading area. Please follow the procedures below to ensure the preservation of the rare and fragile materials housed here.

Library Hours
Open Monday-Friday, 9:00 a.m.-5:00 p.m., and by appointment. Closed weekends, holidays, and scheduled library closings. Summer hours will be posted.

Registration
Butler faculty, staff, and students will be asked to show a current university ID each time they use the collections. Researchers not affiliated with Butler will be asked to fill out a registration form (good for one year) and show a photographic ID for verification. On subsequent visits during the year, you will be asked to show your photographic ID.

Personal Property
Place personal property, including coats, briefcases, purses, backpacks, book bags, computer cases, cellular telephones, and personal audio equipment in the designated area. Food and drink are not permitted in the room. Only materials needed for research, including pencils, paper, and research notes, may be kept with you. Any personal property brought into the room is subject to inspection upon leaving.

Requesting Materials
Most rare books, special collections, and university archives materials are accessible through the online catalog (ILIAD). Collection guides are available for some special collections and for the university archives. Staff members can direct you to the appropriate tools and aid you in finding what you need.

Please fill out a request form, available at the service desk, and give it to the staff member on duty. Since this is a closed stack area, staff will page your materials from the stacks and bring them to the reading area. Please return materials to the staff member at the service desk. Materials will be paged until 4:30 p.m.; all materials must be returned to the service desk by 4:50 p.m. for reshelving.

Handling Materials

Your cooperation in following the procedures below is necessary and appreciated to help preserve materials for future generations of researchers:

- Food and drink are not permitted in the room.
- Use only pencils to take notes; pens are not allowed.
- Handle all materials with care, and follow the instructions given to you by staff. Keep books, bound volumes, manuscripts, and photographs flat on the table. Request book props or stands if you need to hold materials at a more comfortable viewing angle. Except for special weights provided, do not lay any objects on top of library materials. Turn items or pages carefully.
- Maintain all materials in the exact order received.
- You may not trace or scan materials.
- You will be asked to use white cotton gloves when using some materials, including unsleeved photographs and negatives.

Use of Equipment

You may use laptop computers and hand-held cassette tape recorders to take notes. Because of copyright, preservation, and noise considerations, you may not use video cameras or videotaping equipment, still cameras, scanners, cellular phones, or personal audio equipment in the room.

Photocopying

Photocopying can be extremely damaging to rare and fragile materials. We encourage researchers to allow sufficient time to take notes, since this is the least damaging way to carry the information home. You may, however, ask for a photocopy request form at the service desk.

We reserve the right to refuse a photocopy request if filling the request would result in damage to the materials being copied or would violate copyright law. Generally, nothing will be copied in its entirety, and no more than 50 pages or one-third of a collection will be copied, whichever is smaller. Copies are for private study, scholarship, or research use only.

Staff does all photocopying. Requests will be filled as quickly as possible, based on staff time and photocopier access. If necessary, you may be asked to pick up your copies the next day or have them mailed to you.

Photocopying fees are:
10 cents per page for Butler students, faculty, and staff
25 cents per page for researchers not affiliated with Butler

Publication of Collection Materials

"Publish" means the distribution of, or intent to distribute, any number of copies of a work, either by sale or for free. If your use of materials may result in a published work, please inform the staff member at the service desk. You will be asked to complete a *Permission to Publish Contract*. Please note that researchers must obtain all copyright clearances before publishing.

Special Collections, Honnold/Mudd Library, has rich and vast resources in its named collections, Claremont Colleges Archives, rare books, and manuscripts. We invite you to take advantage of these holdings. At the same time, the Special Collections staff has a responsibility to protect and preserve these materials. To reconcile these two important goals, the following rules must govern the use of Special Collections material.

❖ All materials must be used in the Special Collections Reading Room. Books in the Reading Room may be removed from the shelf only by a staff member.

❖ **Only pencil** (no pens), paper and reference materials may be taken to the Readers' table. All other personal property must be stowed on the shelf provided. Staff members will assist in doing this.

❖ You must show your authorized **identification** when calling for an item the first time or on request of a staff member. (Libraries' barcoded card if student, faculty or staff; driver's license or passport if visitor.)

❖ The greatest care must be exercised in handling materials.

❖ Do not write on, lean on, put weights on, or otherwise mishandle material. Uncut leaves of books may be opened only by staff members. Do not erase any marks from books or manuscripts. Pages must be turned gently.

Arrangements may be made to order photocopies and other photographic forms of materials for educational and research purposes, but because of the fragility of some items, all orders will be reviewed by a staff member. Photocopies are 15 cents per sheet if picked up and 25 cents per sheet if mailed. Since all photocopying must be carried out by a staff member, no more than one chapter or 10% of the contents of a book may be photocopied. No material may be removed from Special Collections for photocopying.

Some materials may be scanned at a cost of $40 per hour for large orders, $5 per image for small orders (on disk or printed out), plus the cost of the disk if one is not provided by the researcher. Special Collections reserves the right to refuse to scan large, fragile, and/or brittle material and any material sensitive to light. All orders are subject to approval by Special Collections staff. Three working days advance notice is required for all scanning orders. Please specify black and white or color, resolution (up to 600 dpi/ppi), and file format (tif , gif, jpg, pdf, etc.) Most scans will be made on PC-formatted disks. Other specifications may be arranged with the Digital Projects Specialist.

If you plan to return soon and use the same material, you may request that the items you have been using be placed on hold.

Publication and Copyright

Before any materials from manuscript and photograph collections may be published, permission of the owner(s) of specific collections is obligatory. It is the particular responsibility of the researcher to obtain such permission. The staff will provide the names of owners upon request. Permission to quote from unpublished materials owned by the Libraries of The Claremont Colleges should be requested in writing from: *Librarian, Special Collections, Honnold/Mudd Library, 800 N. Dartmouth Avenue, Claremont, California 91711-3991.* Requests for permission to publish reproductions from rare books and other non-archival printed materials should be directed to the same.

The Copyright Act of 1978 (PL 94-553) provides statutory protection for all writings from the dates of their creation, whether or not they are formally copyrighted. Generally, the term of copyright is the life of the author plus fifty years, but the law also extends copyright protection until December 31, 2002, to all unpublished works now protected under common law. Persons wishing to quote from materials in Special Collections should consult knowledgeable staff members. The Libraries of The Claremont Colleges do hold copyright to some of the manuscript collections and may have information about others. **It is essential that researchers obtain permission for the publication of material not clearly in the public domain, as penalties for violation of this statute are severe.**

Archives & Special Collections @ F&M College Library

Policies and Services

The Archives and Special Collections are available for use by patrons between the hours of 9:00 am - 5:00 pm., Monday through Friday, although specific hours may vary. It is recommended that researchers call in advance to schedule an appointment with the Special Collections Librarian or to confirm current hours.

Policies

- **Collection Development Policy**
- **Gift Policy**
- **Rules for use**

Services

- **Research Assistance**
- **Classroom Instruction**
- **Photocopying**
- **Digital Scanning**

Research Assistance

Research assistance is provided to all visitors of the Archives and Special Collections, as well as to persons inquiring by mail, e-mail, or telephone. While every effort is made to assist in answering one's request, we must limit staff time to twenty minutes for outside requests. For questions regarding the value of your rare book, print, or autograph, please consult our online **Value Guides**.

Classroom Instruction

Classroom instruction is provided in support of the Franklin & Marshall College curriculum. Faculty members are encouraged to contact the Archives & Special Collections to develop specialized instruction sessions utilizing rare and historic materials.

Photocopying

Material can be photocopied for personal use by departmental staff. Due to limitations on staff time, as well as wear and tear on the materials, we may not be able to meet all photocopy requests. In addition, any and all material may be protected under **U.S. Copyright Law** and the department reserves the right to refuse or limit a photocopying request if it appears in clear violation of copyright law.

Charges:
In person, on site: $.10 per page.

By mail:
Charges are $.20 per page with a minimum charge of $2.00 per request to cover postage and staff time. Payment must be received **BEFORE** copies will be mailed. Checks should be made payable to "Franklin and Marshall College" and mailed to:

Archives and Special Collections
Shadek-Fackenthal Library
Franklin and Marshall College
P.O. Box 3003
Lancaster, PA 17604-3003

Sorry, we are unable to accept credit cards at this time.

Digital Scanning

Photographic materials held in the collection may be reproduced for personal use or for use in publications subject to the same regulations governing photocopies or other copyrighted materials.

Charges:
In-House Digital scanning: Documents and photographs can be scanned and sent electronically, or can be scanned and color printed on 8x10 photo glossy paper for a fee of $3.00 including postage.

For multiple images, a CD-ROM can be produced at a cost of $5.00 including shipping and handling.

As in the case of photocopies, payment must be received **BEFORE** any digital scans are mailed.

A **Permission to Use for Publication** form is available to researchers wishing to publish materials from the collections.

NOTICE - WARNING CONCERNING COPYRIGHT RESTRICTIONS

The copyright law of the United States (Title 17, United States Code) governs the making of photocopies or other reproductions of copyrighted materials. Under certain conditions specified in the law, libraries and archives are authorized to furnish a photocopy or other reproduction. One of these specified conditions is that the photocopy or reproduction is not to be "used for any purposes other than private study, scholarship, or research." If a user makes a request for, or later uses, a photocopy or reproduction for purposes in excess of "fair use," that user may be liable for copyright infringement.

This institution reserves the right to refuse to accept a copying order if, in its judgment, fulfillment of the order would involve violation of copyright law. Permission for the reproduction in print of this work or works from the collections (if applicable) is on a one-time only, non-exclusive basis. Franklin &

Marshall retains all future rights to reproduction in publication of its collections. However, Franklin & Marshall College does not claim to control the copyrights of all materials in its collections. Users are solely responsible for determining the ownership of copyrights and for obtaining any permissions which may be necessary for the proposed use. By granting permission to publish, Franklin and Marshall College does not assume any liability for infringement of others copyrights and the user agrees to hold the College harmless from any liability.

Return to top of page

Contact us

rev. 12/18/02

In-House Use Policy

1. Use of materials in the archives reference area is by appointment only during posted archives hours.
2. No materials are to leave the reference area. Archives staff will retrieve the requested materials and deliver them to the reference area for use by the researcher.
3. No food, drink, chewing gum or tobacco products are permitted in the archives reference area.
4. Use pencils only. No ink pens of any type are allowed. If necessary, pencils will be provided by archives staff.
5. Never write on top of documents.
6. No briefcases or backpacks are allowed in the reference area.
7. Only one folder at a time may be used
8. Researchers must take care not to mark, fold, tear or otherwise harm the records in any way. Any damage found by the researcher should be brought to the attention of the archives staff immediately.
9. Never remove items from the folder or rearrange items within the folder.
10. All materials for photocopying need to be reviewed by archives staff to determine that the condition of the document is acceptable for photocopying. The archivist reserves the right to deny permission to photocopy if the document is frail and/or could be permanently damaged due to the procedure.
11. If materials have been approved for photocopying, Researchers will make their own copies if a copier is available in the reference room. In this case, no more than a folder at a time is allowed at the copier, but turning the documents lengthwise to stand up is acceptable for marking copies. If a copier is not available, archives staff will be responsible for making copies and copy slips will be provided to the researcher, who will be responsible for the costs.
12. Researchers are responsible for adhering to United States Copyright Law as incorporated in Title 17 of the United States Code, enacted as public law on October 19, 1976, and subsequent revisions.

I understand the rules for use of the Archives administered by North Central College Library Services and agree to abide by them:

Signed:_____ Date:_____

Name: _____

Address: _____

Phone: _____
Researcher Affiliation:
NCC Faculty/Staff _____ NCC Student _____ NCC Alumni _____ Public _____

Research Topic: _____

cas/kjb
9/03

Ohio Wesleyan University

Libraries & Information Services (LIS)

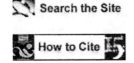

Search the Site

How to Cite

General Use Policy

Definitions

"Archives/Special Collections" as defined in this policy include materials in the Archives of Ohio United Methodism, the Ohio Wesleyan Historical Collection, and the Rare Books, Manuscripts, and Artifacts Collection also known as Special Collections. The "Archives/Special Collections Area" is the secured enclosure on the second floor of Beeghly Library where the Archives/Special Collections are stored.

Access to the Collections

Materials are housed in the Archives/Special Collections Area because they are unique, rare, or of greater value than materials typically owned by the university. Special preservation measures are required in order to continue to make these materials available to Ohio Wesleyan students, faculty, staff, and alumni, as well as outside researchers, including United Methodist Church historians, genealogists, and other interested persons. The goal of any limitation on access to the Archives/Special Collections Area is to strike a balance between user needs and preservation efforts in order to insure the continued availability of the materials to as many users as possible.

Accordingly, access to the Archives/Special Collections Area is limited to those times when Archives/Special Collections staff are available or when the Archives/Special Collections staff have approved unsupervised use of the collections (see Special Users section below). In cases where the text of materials contained in the Archives/Special Collection Area can be obtained elsewhere on campus, users are asked to do so.

Written guidelines regulating the use and handling of Archives/Special Collections materials are provided to users working in the Archives/Special Collections Area. While continued access to the collections is contingent upon compliance with these guidelines, the guidelines, like the access limitations, are in no way intended to discourage use of the collections. Their only purpose is to insure the availability of these materials to future users.

In order to facilitate access to Archives/Special Collections materials staff members are available during scheduled hours and during specially arranged times to plan research strategies and orient users to the Archives/Special Collections card catalogs and other available finding aids.

Hours

Hours of accessibility to all three collections may vary depending upon time of year, time within the academic term, and availability of staff. Hours are posted outside the Archives/Special Collections Area. Every effort is made to maintain consistent hours and to inform users when hours vary.

For reasons of security and statistics those working in the Archives/Special Collections Area are asked to sign in and out.

Circulation and Duplication

Materials housed in the Special Collections Area do not circulate. When warranted by special needs and circumstances the heads of the collections may grant permission to circulate an item and will determine the length of the loan period. In almost all cases, however, materials must be used within the secured Archives/Special Collections Area.

Duplication of materials is permitted provided that copying a given item will not damage the item in any way. Because most materials are fragile, all copying is done by Special Collections staff. Users are charged a specified rate above self-service copying charged because of the special handling involved.

Telephone and Mail Use

Information from materials in the Archives/Special Collection Area may be obtained by telephone or mail request. These requests are processed in keeping with the mission of the collections which generally places a higher emphasis on service to the campus and scholarly community. Priority is also given to use by The United Methodist Church in the case of the Archives of Ohio United Methodism and use by the alumni in the case of the Ohio Wesleyan University Historical Collection. In all cases service to community groups and to those studying the history of their family are given secondary priority.

Where significant staff time is required to research requests for family history, a research fee may be charged. A research fee may also be charged when scholars require work demanding significant staff time rather than incur travel costs.

Visitor Categories

General Users

Those wishing to use the Archives/Special collections for short periods of time are referred to as "general users" and are urged to make an appointment so that staff will be available and prepared to assist them.

General users seeking access to the Special Collections Area at times when Archives/Special Collections staff members are not available regrettably can not be assisted but should be asked by library staff to fill out a research request form so that service can be arranged at a mutually convenient time. Likewise, users seeking information over the telephone when Archives/Special Collections staff are not available should be encouraged to leave a message detailing their research request.

Special Users

Users needing extended periods of access may be granted Special User status for a designated period of time. Criteria for designation as a Special User include:
1. demonstrated understanding of and respect for the guidelines for use of materials,
2. legitimate need to use the collections at times other than when staff are present, and,
3. work on projects requiring sustained use of the collections for scholarly, university, or church-related work.

This status is granted by those in charge of the respective collections after consultation with the user. Special Users are permitted to obtain a key to the Special Collections area during regular library hours when the Special Collections Area is unsupervised by signing in at the Circulation Desk.

Scholars-in-Residence

Users may also be granted Scholar-in-Residence status for renewable one-term periods. Those granted this status are scholars, including OWU students and faculty, who have continuous need for the resources in the collections and are conducting research which requires a greater level of support than that of Special Users. In addition to the criteria for Special User status, those granted scholar-in-Residence status must be working on a significant project such as a book, dissertation, or independent study. Scholars-in-Residence are issued keys to the Special Collections Area, and provided with work space, inter-library loan services, online searching, and other services as needed and as appropriate for the duration of the term.

Scholars-in-Residence may have access to the Special Collections Area any time the library is open, with the exception of Sunday-Thursday from 11 p.m.-12 a.m. Special Users and Scholars-in-

Residence, like other users, are asked to sign in and out.

Group Visitors

Visits to the Archives/Special Collections area by classes, confirmation classes, community groups, etc., are encouraged within the limits of preservation mandates. Prior arrangement must be made with the appropriate Archives/Special Collections staff member and a list of visitors supplied at the time of the visit for security purposes.

OWU LIS is a member of

OhioLINK   Five Colleges of Ohio

Last updated on August 16, 2004
Send questions & comment to Web Manager
© 2004, Ohio Wesleyan University Libraries & Information Services (LIS)

43 Rowland Ave.
Delaware, OH 43015
Telephone: 740-368-3225 Fax: 740-368-3222

Ouachita Baptist University

THE LIBRARY

Riley-Hickingbotham Library at Ouachita Baptist University

. . . .

Policies Governing Special Collections Use

General Provisions

SITE INDEX
baptist records
books & rare books
ccha publications
county records
manuscripts
maps
newspapers
oral histories
policies
regional studies
photographs
request forms
contact us

Special Collections of Riley-Hickingbotham Library of Ouachita Baptist University is the institution's official archives, responsible for collecting, preserving and providing access to collections of unique materials which require special care. It also serves as the official repository for the Clark County Historical Association and the Arkansas Baptist State Convention. All three major divisions contain resources concerning persons and events significant to that entity's past. To ensure the preservation of those materials, Special Collections never loans materials to anyone for any reason.

Access to Materials. Access is generally granted to anyone with a legitimate claim to use material for scholarly or other responsible purposes, but no material from any collection will be made available to a user until the prescribed application form has been completed, signed and approved. Special Collections materials may not be browsed. Researchers are encouraged to consult any available finding aids and the Archivist before undertaking research in the Library's collections. Access to an excessive quantity of material is not permitted.

Use of Material for Publication. Researchers assume all responsibility for abiding by the provisions of Copyright Law. Neither receiving access to, nor copies of, materials in a collection convey or imply conveyance of the right to publish such materials or to quote extensively from them in publication. Researchers planning publication who are not familiar with statutory and common law literary property rights and other legal aspects involved in quoting from or reproducing the contents of unpublished material are advised to consult with an attorney.

Citing of Collections. Any work based on research in one or more of the Library's manuscript collections must properly cite the source or sources used, naming the collection as well as Special Collections, Riley-Hickingbotham Library, Ouachita Baptist University.

54 Access and Use Policies

Submission of one copy of each publication which utilizes material from Special Collections is required.

Copying. Researchers may not electronically scan any item. Requests for extensive copying cannot be accommodated. In some instances, selected documents from some collections may, depending on a number of considerations, be reproduced for researchers. Requests to copy a limited quantity (not to exceed 50 pages) of specific documents from a particular collection may be presented to the Archivist or deputy, who may approve or deny the request in whole or in part. Approved copying will be arranged and handled by the staff. Payment for copying must be made in advance unless deferred payment is arranged.

Exceptions. No exceptions to these policies will be made. Anyone violating Library policies will lose use privileges.

Policy Governing Use of Manuscript Collections

Restrictions. Access to collections subject to specific restrictions requires prior consultation with the Archivist. Approved access to a specific collection or collections does not convey unlimited access; specific documents may remain restricted.

Security Requirements and Restrictions. Researchers are only permitted to have a pencil and notepaper or cards and/or a computer on or near the table at which manuscript material is examined. All pens, books, briefcases, handbags, file folders, papers (other than notepaper or cards) and other possessions, including overgarments, carried into the reading room by a researcher must be placed in a designated temporary storage area. All material from manuscript collections must be handled and used only with the greatest care. Documents must be subjected to a minimum of handling and must at all times, except when filed in shelf container, lie flat on the table at which they are being examined. No marks of any kind are to be made on the face or verso of any document, and no document is to be creased or folded in any manner other than that in which it is normally shelved. Access may be limited to transcripts, microform, or photocopies only of especially fragile or valuable documents where such transcripts or photocopies are, or can be made, available, and where their use is, in the opinion of staff personnel, sufficient for the researcher's purpose. Staff personnel will at all times oversee researcher's use of manuscript materials. Materials may be subject to checking by a staff member and before leaving the reading room, researchers may be asked to submit notes and other papers for examination.

Quantities of Material. Staff members will provide only a limited number of folders or single documents, to a maximum of one shelf container, for a researcher at a time. When the researcher has finished with those materials, a staff member will replace them with additional materials as requested. Researchers are required to preserve the exact order of all documents in each folder or container made available to them.

Use of Material for Publication. In many cases, the university Library's rights to material in its manuscript collections extends only to the physical documents, and not to the contents of the documents. In all cases, the literary rights to incoming correspondence in a collection, or to any document not written or produced by the creator of the collection, remain the property of the original author or producer or his heirs or assignees. The Library cannot guarantee publication rights and assumes no responsibility for a researcher's use or misuse of the contents of documents made available to or copied for him under terms of its established policies governing access to its collections.

Policy Governing Use of Photographic Materials

Copies of photographs/visuals are available from The Library upon completion of a photograph reproduction form and its return along with payment for the total cost. All fees must be paid before any order can be processed. All photograph orders will be handled directly by The Library. Negatives will not be supplied to patrons, and they may not arrange for work to be done by an outside person or agency. Patrons may not reproduce photographs/visuals by any means in any format without the express written consent of The Library. The Library reserves the right to refuse to honor requests for photographic reproduction.

Policy Governing Use of Audiovisual Materials

Special Collections contains audio and video tapes of events, and interviews with individuals about events, pertinent to all three of its major divisions. Researchers are required to use transcripts when available for their initial access to audiovisual material. When researchers are granted access to audio or video tapes, they may only use one at the time and must utilize equipment provided by the Library. Personal recording devices may not be used and should not be present in the research area. Approved access to specific audiovisual material conveys no publication rights to a researcher. In some instances, copies of audiovisual materials or transcripts may be provided. Such provision is strictly for a researcher's convenience and conveys no publication rights. Researchers may not make copies of any materials; any approved copying will be done by staff personnel at the researcher's expense. All attendant fees must be paid prior to any copying unless deferred payment is arranged. Special Collections will not copy an excessive number of audiovisual materials for a researcher.

Contact Us

Ms. Wendy Richter, archivist
OBU Box 3729
Arkadelphia, AR 71998
richterw@obu.edu
870.245.5332

. . . .

Library Home • E-Mail the Library Webmaster • Last Updated May 2003

The University of Tennessee at Martin
Paul Meek Library
Special Collections/Univ. Archives
Service Policies

The Jimmie and Alliene Corbitt Special Collections and Archives (the Collection) is a departmental unit of the Paul Meek Library on the campus of the University of Tennessee at Martin. As a unit, Special Collections' mission is to identify, acquire, preserve, and make available to its readership documentary materials of archival value relative to the University of Tennessee at Martin and its predecessor, and similar historical and cultural materials which fall under the venues of its other four respective sections: Rare books and book collections; Tennessee and regional history; Genealogy, and Manuscripts.

Readership

The Collection serves several constituent readerships. Its primary service is directed to the students, faculty and staff of the institution. A secondary mission is to serve the historical and genealogical interests of the public in western Tennessee outside of Memphis. A third constituency comprises all others who may come to the Collection seeking to use materials housed there.

The Collection is open to all users willing to abide by the library and unit service policies. Any reader choosing not to use material within the established rules will be refused service at the Curator's discretion.

Point of Service

Materials from the book collections (including rare books), Manuscripts, and University archives (including photos), are available to researchers only as closed-stack, non-circulating holdings and must be used within the Reading Room. Retrieval requests may be made to Special Collections staff between 8am and 4:30pm. weekdays, or by special prior arrangement with the Curator, and at no other time. All material must be returned to the hands of Collections staff fifteen minutes before closing (typically 4:45pm).

+ Patrons will place carriable bags and cases in the lockers beside the circulation desk.
+ Pencils may be used to take notes while working with materials; ink of any sort may not be used.
+ Photocopies may be made for patrons by departmental staff at the discretion of the Curator; duplication may be refused if it would compromise the long-term physical integrity of an item.
+ Materials will be returned to the hands of a Special Collections staff member before leaving.

Materials in the West Tennessee Heritage Study Center are available for research as open-stack, non-circulating materials that must be used within the confines of its room. This collections is available during general library service hours, on the following conditions:

+ Patrons will place carriable bags and cases in the lockers beside the circulation desk. None are allowed in the Tennessee room.
+ Patrons will sign the registration ledger and deposit a piece of photo identification at the circulation desk prior to admittance, and will be admitted by library circulation or Special Collections personnel.
+ The door to the collections must remain locked from the outside. Patrons may leave at will but must ask to be readmitted.
+ Pencils may be used to take notes while working with WTHSC materials; ink of any sort may not be used.
+ Do not mark the pages of collection materials in any way.
+ All materials must remain in the WTHSC room. Books should be left on the tables and not reshelved; microfilm in their boxes should be left atop the microfilm cabinets.

<u>Reproductions</u>

Patrons may not themselves photocopy any materials from the Collection. All requests for reproductions from unit holdings are subject to approval by the Curator. Reproduction may be refused if: 1) the physical preservation of an item could be threatened by reproduction; 2) the general fair-use terms governed by Title 17 of the U.S. Code would be infringed; 3) there is a legal, statutory, administrative, or terms-of-gift restriction limiting or prohibiting reproduction.

Photocopies   Reproductions from monographic works are made only by library staff. Patrons must complete a photocopy order form to be placed in the item to be photocopied. Photocopies will be available for pickup the following day or may be mailed for an additional charge. Payment must be made through the library circulation desk.

Patrons may make their own photocopies at will from microfilm on the coin-operated reader/printer in the WTHSC room. Please be careful.

Photographs and digital reproductions   [in process]

WILLIAMS COLLEGE ARCHIVES & SPECIAL COLLECTIONS

RULES GOVERNING USE OF THE COLLECTIONS

Our department exists to preserve the heritage of the past and to make it available to researchers. Our regulations, therefore, are designed to ensure the careful preservation of our collections. We solicit your assistance in this endeavor.

The Archives and Special Collections reading room, located in the Mabie Room in Stetson Hall, is open Monday through Friday, 10:00 a.m. to 12:00 noon and 1:00 to 4:45 p.m. (Summer hours may vary.)

Registration
Readers are required to complete a registration form upon which will be logged all materials used. All coats, briefcases, bags and backpacks must be deposited with Archives staff. Access to certain collections may be governed by restrictions placed on the materials by their donors or depositors, or by the physical condition of the material.

Protection of collections
Care should be taken in the examination of all collections. No materials may be removed from the reading room, and the original order of all manuscripts and folders must be maintained. The use of any kind of pen is prohibited. The collections may not be written upon, traced, or handled in any way likely to damage them. Eating and smoking are not permitted in the reading room.

Photoduplication
All photocopying will be done by the Archives staff, and is subject to their restrictions. Reproductions are made for research purposes only, and may not be transferred to any other person or institution without prior written permission of the College Archivist.

Permission to publish
Separate written application for permission to publish original material must be made to the College Archivist. Researchers will assume full responsibility for obtaining the necessary publication rights and copyright clearances. In granting permission to publish, the Archives does not surrender its own right thereafter to publish the material or to grant permission to others to publish it; nor does the Library assume any responsibility for infringement of copyright.

If you have any questions regarding these rules or our collections, please feel free to speak with the Archives staff.

XAVIER UNIVERSITY LIBRARIES
ARCHIVES AND SPECIAL COLLECTIONS GUIDELINES

Archives and Special Collections are unique collections of the University Libraries. Their fragile and irreplaceable condition requires stringent monitoring and careful handling. Every care is made to protect and preserve these collections. The following guidelines are set to this end.

- Access to these collections is by <u>advanced</u> appointment only.
- All and any requests (in person, electronically, or by telephone or letter) for Archives or Special Collections materials will be directed to Tim McCabe (Telephone Number: 513-745-4821; Fax Number 513-745-1932; E-Mail: mccabe@xu.edu; Mailing address: Xavier University Libraries, 3800 Victory Parkway, Cincinnati, Ohio 45207-5211). Alternately, Archives staff may be reached at 513-745-2805.
- Response to these requests will be handled as quickly as possible, consistent with <u>the appropriateness of a patron's request, legitimate scholarly intent, and an absence of confidentiality issues</u>. Every effort will be made to respond to requests within two weeks.
- Access to the Archives and Special Collections is restricted to library staff <u>designated by the Library Director</u>. Staff may invite a patron to enter the collections area under extenuating situations. <u>PATRONS ARE NOT TO BE LEFT ALONE IN ARCHIVES OR SPECIAL COLLECTIONS</u>.
- Patrons may be required to complete a "Archives/Special Collections Patron Registration Form" prior to using the collections. In addition, positive identification may be kept (e.g. driver's license) while patrons use the materials.
- <u>Special Collections materials do not circulate. Archival materials may circulate to university personnel for due cause under extraordinary and safeguarded conditions. Letters of conveyance accompany an archival loan. Such letters detail the items loaned, the date items are due, and the borrower (name, address, telephone number).</u> Copies of these letters are kept on file.
- In-library use of these materials will be under the direct supervision/monitoring of the <u>designated</u> library staff member. Materials will be available for patron use normally in the Library Conference Room on the First Floor. Use of materials are subject to the following guidelines:
  - Patrons may not eat, drink, or use tobacco products while Special Collections/Archival materials are in use. Chewing gum is also prohibited.
  - No pencil or other object of any kind ma be held in the hand while pages of Special Collections/Archival materials are in use.
  - Only materials needed for research may be taken into the viewing area. Briefcases, handbags and computer cases as well as coats and hats are not allowed in the viewing area. All personal effects are subject to inspection prior to and following patrons viewing materials.
  - Under no circumstances are marks of any kind to be made in the materials.

- The only objects that may be placed in materials are acid-free markers available at the Library.
- No books or other materials are to be placed on top of materials. Tracings may not be made from materials.
- Patrons must use pencils only while working with materials. Handling of materials is to be kept to a minimum.
- Materials will be viewed in a controlled manner. No more than two volumes will be viewed at one time, or in the case of Archival materials, the "one box, one folder" rule will be used. All materials are to be viewed flat on the table.
- Photocopying of materials is discouraged and may be done only at the discretion of the library staff member. Fragile materials will not be photocopied. Patrons are liable for any copyright infringement. All photocopying is to be done by a library staff member with the expense the responsibility of the requestor (50 cents per exposure).
- **THE LIBRARY RESERVES THE RIGHT TO DENY ACCESS TO THESE MATERIALS OR TO MODIFY THESE GUIDELINES AS NEEDED DUE TO THE CONDITION OF MATERIALS AND/OR STAFF AVAILABILITY.**

12/2/2000

READER REGISTRATION FORMS

BOWDOIN COLLEGE LIBRARY
George J. Mitchell Department of Special Collections & Archives
Reader Registration Form

(Please print)
Last name, First name:

_____

Address: _____

_____

_____

Phone: ( ) _____

Staff use only:
Approved:_____
Date: _____
ID:_____
_____

Institutional Affiliation:_____

Research Status (*choose one*):

( ) Bowdoin Student ( ) Bowdoin Faculty ( ) Bowdoin Staff ( ) Bowdoin Alum

( ) Other Student ( ) Other Faculty ( ) Independent Scholar ( ) _____ *(Other)*

Research Interest:_____

May we mention your name and address to others with similar research interests? (*please initial*) _____ Yes _____ No

I have read and agree to abide by the Rules for Readers printed below:

1. Because Special Collections & Archives materials are rare, fragile, unique, or of special collecting interest, they may be consulted only in the department Reading Room under departmental supervision.
2. All readers who can furnish a photographic form of identification (*e.g.*, student ID, driver's license) and who agree to abide by these rules may use the collections; grade school students must be accompanied by a supervising adult.
3. No personal belongings, including backpacks, purses, book bags, coats, and notebooks, are permitted in the Reading Room. Readers may bring laptop computers into the Reading Room, but computer travel bags/cases are not permitted. Please place these belongings in the storage area provided for them.
4. The use of ink is not permitted. Nor may the reader make any marks on any departmental materials. In taking notes, please do not rest notepaper directly on books or manuscripts; tracing is not permitted. The department supplies notepaper and pencils as needed.
5. All materials must be handled with care. Maintain loose papers in the order in which they are received. Please bring apparent filing irregularities to our attention, but do not attempt to rearrange manuscript collections or archival records personally. Some of our books have uncut pages; please bring these to our attention as you encounter them so that we may open them for you.
6. Limited photocopying is possible depending on the fragility of particular items and compliance with copyright law. All requests for copies are subject to departmental review. Copies are prepared by department staff following the posted schedule for copying charges. Photocopies are made for private study, scholarship or research only; under no circumstance may copies of materials from our collections be deposited in another repository or institution without our express written permission.
7. Any reader wishing to publish from Special Collections & Archives materials agrees to obtain permission prior to publication from the Director of Special Collections & Archives, from all holders of copyright, and from other interested parties as applicable. The reader agrees to accept full responsibility for complying with laws enacted to protect copyright and privacy rights. The department is obliged to deny access to materials that are protected under the Family Educational Rights and Privacy Act and other relevant privacy laws.

_____   _____

Signature   Date

REGISTRATION FORM
For Researchers Not Affiliated with Butler University
Special Collections and Rare Books
Butler University Libraries

Date:_____

Name:_____

Address:_____

_____

Phone:_____ Fax:_____ E-Mail_____

Institutional/Corporate affiliation:_____

Address:_____

_____

Phone:_____ Fax:_____ E-Mail_____

Local contact information:_____

_____

Photo ID (type and number):_____

Research interests:

_____
_____
_____
_____
_____
_____
_____
_____

Staff notes:

_____
_____
_____
_____
_____
_____
_____

COLORADO COLLEGE
1 8 7 4

Colorado College

Special Collections, Tutt Library
Application to Use Manuscript Materials

Date_____

Name_____ Phone_____

Address_____

Institution_____ Email _____

CC status (circle one if applicable): Student Faculty Administration Staff

_____
I.D. number (gold card, driver's license, passport)

[Photocopy I.D. here]

Permission to examine manuscript materials is granted *for reference purposes only*. It does not include permission to reproduce or publish materials.

Permission for reproductions is granted *for reference purposes only*. Information about fees for photocopies, scans, and reproductions is available from Special Collections staff.

I understand the rules governing use of Special Collections and by my signature indicate that I agree to abide by them.

_____   _____
Signature   Staff initials

TUTT LIBRARY
1021 North Cascade Avenue, Colorado Springs, Colorado 80903-3252
719-389-6000 *tel* 719-389-6859 *fax*
www.ColoradoCollege.edu/Library

Reader Registration Forms 67

Fort Valley State University

HOMIE REGULUS HERITAGE ARCHIVES
Fort Valley State University

Registration Form

Date: _____

Name: _____

Local Address: _____

Permanent Address: _____

Telephone: Local: _____ Permanent: _____

School/University: _____

Undergraduate: _____ Graduate: _____ Faculty: _____ Other: _____

Leave your ID at the desk: _____

Archives Personnel Use Only

Subject of Research: _____

Publication Plans: _____

Search Approved for Restricted Materials: _____ Date: _____

Materials Available: _____

_____

_____

_____

_____

Personal Contact: _____   Mail: _____   Telephone: _____

MASSACHUSETTS COLLEGE OF THE LIBERAL ARTS
SPECIAL COLLECTIONS

NAME _____   DATE _____

ADDRESS _____

_____

NATURE OF RESEARCH:

     ADMINISTRATIVE INQUIRY _____   THESIS _____

     RESEARCH PAPER: _____ UNDERGRADUATE
                        _____ GRADUATE

     OTHER: _____

PATRON DESCRIPTION:

     MCLA FACULTY _____   MCLA STAFF ADMIN. _____

     MCLA UNDERGRAD. _____   MCLA GRAD. STUDENT _____

     OTHER EDUC. INSTITUTION _____

     GOVT. AGENCY _____   GENERAL PUBLIC _____

(TO BE COMPLETED BY LIBRARY STAFF)

ITEMS LOANED FOR USE: (LIST CALL #, TITLE, DATE, AND BRIEF DESCRIPTION)

REGULATIONS FOR USE OF MCLA ARCHIVAL MATERIALS:

1. ALL MATERIALS MUST BE USED ON THE MAIN FLOOR OF THE LIBRARY.
2. SOME FORM OF IDENTIFICATION IS REQUIRED (STUDENT ID, DRIVER'S LICENSE)
3. NO MARKS ARE TO BE MADE ON MATERIALS.
4. NO FOOD OR BEVERAGES ARE TO BE USED WHILE HANDLING DOCUMENTS.
5. THE RESEARCHER WILL MAINTAIN THE DOCUMENTS IN THE ORDER THEY ARE RECEIVED.
6. THE DOCUMENTS ARE TO BE RETURNED TO THE CIRCULATION DESK OR AN AVAILABLE REFERENCE LIBRARIAN.
7. THE RESEARCHER IS ADVISED THAT MCLA DOESN NOT HOLD THE LITERARY RIGHTS TO THE MATERIALS IN ITS COLLECTIONS AND THAT IT IS THE RESEARCHER'S RESPONSIBILITY TO SECURE THOSE RIGHTS WHEN NEEDED.

THE RESEARCHER BY SIGNING THIS FORM ACKNOWLEDGES HIS/HER RESPONSIBILITY TO OBSERVE THE ABOVE REGULATIONS AND FURTHER ACKNOWLEDGES THAT A VIOLATION OF THESE REGULATIONS WILL SERVE AS CAUSE TO PROHIBIT HIS/HER CONFIRMED USE OF MCLA ARCHIVE MATERIALS.

_____
PATRON'S SIGNATURE

North Central College

Researcher Information

Name: _____

Address: _____

Phone: _____

Researcher Affiliation:
NCC Faculty/Staff _____ NCC Student _____ NCC Alumni _____ Public _____

On-site _____ Phone _____ Letter _____ Email _____

Administrative _____ Thesis/Dissertation _____ Course work _____
Historical research _____ Personal Interest _____ Genealogy _____
Publication _____

Research Subject: _____

_____

Date: _____

Result of Research: _____

Materials used:
<u>Record Group #</u>   Box # _____   <u>Description</u> _____

APPLICATION FOR THE USE OF MANUSCRIPTS AND ORIGINAL MATERIALS
HELD IN THE SPECIAL COLLECTIONS OF
WELLESLEY COLLEGE LIBRARY
WELLESLEY, MASSACHUSETTS 02181

Name_____ Date_____

Address_____ Position/Affiliation_____

_____ _____

I hereby request permission to examine the following manuscript or original materials:

for the purpose of (a specific statement of your topic is required):

I understand that permission to examine a manuscript or original materials, if granted, does not include permission to publish the contents of the manuscript or original materials at any time, and that separate written application for permission to publish must be made to the Special Collections Librarian, specifying the manuscript or original materials. I agree to abide by her decision.

I understand further that the College makes no representation that it is the owner of the copyright or literary property in any unpublished manuscript or original materials unless otherwise stated, and that permission to publish must also be obtained from the owner of the copyright (the author, or his/her transferees, heirs, legatees or literary executors).

If this application includes a request for xerox, microfilm or other reproduction of any manuscript or original materials listed above on this sheet, I agree that the reproduction is to be made solely for my convenience in examining the manuscripts or original materials; that it is to be returned upon completion of my research; that the reproduction will not itself be reproduced; and that it will not be examined by or transferred to any other person or institution without the prior written permission of the Special Collections Librarian of the Wellesley College Library.

In consideration of my being granted permission to examine any manuscript or original materials on the terms set forth above, I agree to indemnify and hold harmless the College, its officers, employees and agents from and against all claims made by any person asserting that he or she is an owner of the copyright or literary property.

Signature_____

___ Check here if you do **not** wish the Special Collections staff to make anyone else aware of the topic of your research.

Action by Special Collections:

c:\mhatch\invntry\photo.for

MATERIALS REQUEST FORMS

MATERIALS REQUEST FORM
Special Collections and Rare Books
Butler University Libraries

Name:_____Status:_____

Address:_____

City, State, Zip:_____ Phone:_____

Call Number	Author/Title/Collection Name	Out by	Ret. to	Copy

PROCEDURES FOR USING SPECIAL COLLECTIONS AND RARE BOOKS MATERIALS

In order to help preserve these materials, please observe the following:
1. Use pencil only for taking notes; do not mark on any materials.
2. All materials must be used in the reading area. Please return all materials to the staff member at the desk.
3. Exercise care in handling special collections and rare books materials and follow any special instructions given to you by the staff member at the desk.
4. Maintain materials in their original order. If something seems to be out of order, please notify a staff member.

I have read and agree to follow the above procedures for special collections and rare books materials:

Signature:_____Date:_____

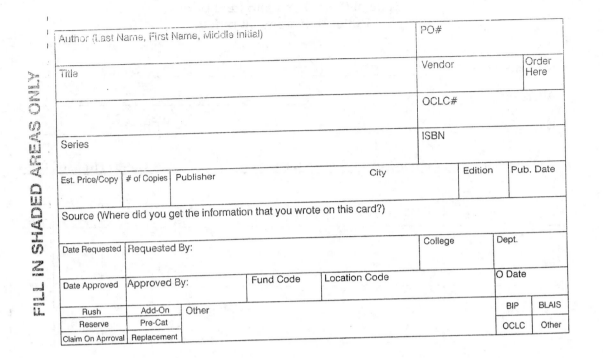

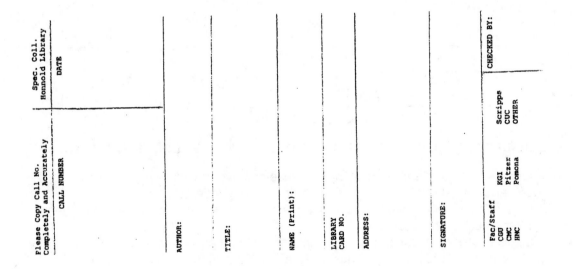

EASTERN WASHINGTON UNIVERSITY
ARCHIVES & SPECIAL COLLECTIONS
SECTION: ___ ERA
___ EWU
___ SPC

RESEARCH APPLICATION
REQUEST FOR ARCHIVAL RECORDS
(Reference: RCW 42.17)

DATE:

TOTAL TIME:

NAME OF REQUESTOR	ADDRESS	TELEPHONE

RESEARCH PROJECT TITLE AND/OR DESCRIPTION

DESCRIPTION OF RECORDS REQUESTED

RECORD GROUP NUMBER & TITLE	SUB-GROUP NUMBER & TITLE	RECORDS SERIES NUMBER & TITLE	OTHER DESCRIPTORS (AS APPLICABLE)

SIGNATURE OF REQUESTOR	DATE/TIME

SSA-52 77

FOR OFFICE USE ONLY

1.
[ ] REQUEST GRANTED   [ ] REQUEST WITHHELD   [ ] REQUEST WITHHELD IN PART

2. IF WITHHELD, NAME THE EXEMPTION CONTAINED IN PARAGRAPH 31, CHAPTER 1, LAWS OF 1973, WHICH AUTHORIZES THE WITH-HOLDING OF THE RECORD OR PART OF THE RECORD. SUBSECTION (1), ( )

3. IF WITHHELD, BRIEFLY EXPLAIN HOW THE EXEMPTION APPLIES TO THE RECORD WITHHELD

4. REFERENCE SERVICES

A. WRITTEN RESEARCH SERVICES	NUMBER OF LETTERS RECEIVED	NUMBER OF LETTERS SENT		
B. DIRECT RESEARCH SERVICES	NUMBER OF TELEPHONE CALLS	NUMBER OF VISITORS		
C. ITEMS FURNISHED FOR REFERENCE	NO. OF VOLUMES	NO. OF FOLDERS	NO. OF BOXES	
	NO. OF DOCUMENTS			
D. OTHER MEDIA FURNISHED FOR RESEARCH	NUMBER OF MICROFILMS	NUMBER OF AUDIO TAPES		
E. COPIES FURNISHED	NUMBER OF PAGES	NUMBER OF MICROFILMS	NUMBER OF TAPES	
F. DOCUMENTS CERTIFIED	NUMBER OF CERTIFICATES			
DATE	TIME	STATE ARCHIVIST OR STAFF MEMBER		

University of South Carolina

Time Loaned: _____

Initials: _____

Time returned: _____

Initials: _____

Special Collections & Rare Books   University of South Carolina

Request Slip

Call Number: _____

Author: _____

Title: _____

Users Name and Address: _____
(Please Print)

_____

Date borrowed: _____ Date returned: _____

Check one: _____ Faculty/Staff _____ Student _____ Visitor

The South Caroliniana Library

CALL SLIP

For stack book, newspaper, map or periodical
(to be used in Reading Room only).

Call Number: s.c.

. . . .

. . . .

. . . .

Author:

Title:

Borrower's name *and address:*

Check one:

Faculty ☐   Student ☐   Other ☐

MANUSCRIPT REQUEST FORM — SOUTH CAROLINIANA LIBRARY

Name of Collection: _____

Letter(s) appearing in upper lefthand corner of catalog card (i.e., P, Plb, I&Oo): _____

Document Type (MSS, Vol. bd., etc.): _____

Date(s) or date span requested: _____

Total number of items requested: _____

Your name: _____
(please print)

Date: _____

All blanks must be filled in if we are to locate the material which you are requesting. You may request only one collection and document type per card. Your assistance is appreciated.

Application for the Examination of Holdings

I hereby request permission to use the holdings in the Widener University Archives. I have read and agree to abide by the regulations.

With respect to copyright and right-to-privacy laws, I personally assume full responsibility for obtaining the necessary publication rights and clearances for any publication that may result from my research. I also agree to acknowledge in the publication the source of the materials used.

I agree that any photographic or any other photoduplication of materials in the Widener University Archives is solely for my personal use, and that said reproduction(s) will not be photoduplicated nor transferred to any other individual or institution without the prior written consent of the Widener University Archives.

Should this research become a significant or major source for a publication, I agree that a copy of the said publication will be presented to the Widener University Archives.

Signature _____

Name _____
(please print)   Last   First   Initial

Permanent Address _____

Permanent Telephone Number _____

Local Address_____
                        (if different from above)

Local Telephone Number _____

USER DESCRIPTION

_____   Widener Faculty or Staff – Department _____

_____   Widener Student – Major _____

_____   Widener Alumni _____

_____   Other Academic Institution _____

_____   General Public _____

NATURE OF RESEARCH
_____   Research Paper
_____   Publication
_____   Administration
_____   Other (please specify)_____

Subject of Research _____

Archives' Staff Member _____ Date _____

WIDENER UNIVERSITY ARCHIVES

REQUEST FOR INFORMATION

Name:_____Today's Date: _____

Phone Number: _____

Address: _____

_____

Access to the Widener University Archives is by appointment only. Call 610-499-4591 or 610-499-4376 to make an appointment to use the Archives. If you are unable to come to the Archives when an Archivist is available, we will do everything we can to accommodate your research needs. Please write below the kind of information you are interested in obtaining from the Archives, being as specific as possible. Please give us any relevant dates and any other information would be helpful to us. We will search for the information you are requesting, photocopy what we find whenever possible, and mail it to you.

Type of Information Requested:

_____

_____

_____

_____

_____

_____

_____

_____

_____

_____

_____

REPROGRAPHICS, POLICIES, AND RELATED FORMS

BOWDOIN COLLEGE LIBRARY
George J. Mitchell Department of Special Collections & Archives
Duplication Policy

All duplicating of Special Collections & Archives materials is done by Library staff. Materials may be copied (photomechanically, magnetically or digitally) when, in the judgement of the staff, such copying will not damage the original item(s), will not duplicate an inordinate portion of a manuscript collection, archival record group or bound volume, and is not prohibited by US copyright law. While the Library makes every attempt to accommodate copying requests, making copies is inherently stressful to the original(s). Consequently, limits have been established to balance researchers' needs and our obligation to preserve these special resource materials. To reduce stress on bindings, all photocopying of bound volumes is limited to no more than twenty (20) pages per volume. Some items, such as brittle, tightly bound or heavy books, are impossible to photocopy. Sometimes, alternative photoduplication (*e.g.*, microfilming, photography) are suitable when electrostatic copying is infeasible. Readers wanting to copy a substantial portion of a manuscript collection, a group of College records, or a published work may be asked to pay instead for the production of a microfilm copy of the entire portion.

Special conditions apply when requesting duplication of unpublished materials. Virtually all unpublished manuscripts, recordings, and photographs are protected under copyright law. Select photocopies of manuscripts may be made if they are solely for the research use of the applicant; further photoduplication of such copies is not permitted, nor may those copies be deposited in another institution. Nor does Bowdoin College Library, in making research copies available, thereby grant permission to reproduce those copies or to quote extensively from them for publication. In making use of these copies, the applicant assumes full responsibility for any infringement of copyright or publication rights belonging to the author, the author's heirs or assigns. The applicant also accepts responsibility for communicating with the holder(s) of copyright concerning permissions to quote or otherwise publish material protected by copyright from our collections. Special copyright provisions apply to sound recordings, pictorial, musical, graphic, motion picture, or other audio-visual works that severely restrict duplicating without the express permission of the holder of copyright.

Publishing material from our holdings requires permission not only from the holders of copyright but also from Bowdoin College Library. For permission to publish, please write to the Director, George J. Mitchell Department of Special Collections & Archives, Bowdoin College Library, 3000 College Stations, Brunswick, Maine 04011-8421. A publication fee may apply.

The department fills orders as quickly as possible. Requests from resident researchers take precedence; research requests received through the mail, by phone or electronically will be handled as time, the availability of staff, and the fragility of the material allows. In all instances, a signed Request for Duplication is prerequisite to filling any duplication order.

The applicant agrees to pay the costs incurred in making all requested copies following established fee schedules, including expenses in preparing negatives and file copies retained by the department. Orders that require photographic, magnetic or digital copying, and mail orders require prepayment. We regret that we cannot provide billing for non-Bowdoin College accounts.

> Cost of photocopies:
> $ .10 per exposure for in-house requests
> $ .25 per exposure for mail-order requests ($2.50 minimum)

For other duplication service costs, please consult our fee schedule.

Mail orders require prepayment, including a $5.00 service charge for mailing/handling. Payments by check or money order are payable to "**Bowdoin College.**"

Rev. 2/02

BOWDOIN COLLEGE LIBRARY
George J. Mitchell Department of Special Collections & Archives
Request for Duplication

Address of Applicant *(Please print)*

Name _____

Street _____

City _____ State _____ Zip _____

Phone _____ Email _____

Date of Request _____ Date Needed _____

( ) Pickup   ( ) Mail [$5.00]   ( ) Campus Mail   ( ) Campus charge

Campus account no._____

Please indicate
form of duplication:

( ) Photocopy
( ) Photograph
  ( ) B/W Size:_____
  ( ) Col. Size:_____
  ( ) Transparency
( ) Digital file
  Specs:_____

( ) Other:_____

Notice: Warning Concerning Copyright Restrictions

The copyright law of the United States (*Title 17, United States Code*) governs the making of photocopies or other reproductions of copyrighted material.

Under certain conditions specified in the law, libraries and archives are authorized to furnish a photocopy or other reproduction. One of these specified conditions is that the photocopy or reproduction is not to be "used for any purpose other than private study, scholarship, or research." If the user makes a request for, or later uses a photocopy or reproduction for purposes in excess of "fair use," that user may be liable for copyright infringement.

This institution reserves the right to refuse to accept a copying order if, in its judgment, fulfillment of the order would involve violation of copyright law.

I have read the above restrictions and the Special Collections & Archives Duplication Policy on the reverse of this form, and I make application for duplication of the material listed below:

_____   _____
Signature   Date

Call Number	Author/Title	Portions to be Copied

Staff use only:
  No. expos._____ x $._____ = $_____ + Svc/Mailing Chrg. $ _____ + Tax $ _____ = TOTAL $ _____

  Approved: _____ Date: _____   Completed by: _____ Date: _____

Special Collections & Archives, Bowdoin College Library, 3000 College Station, Brunswick, ME 04011-8421
Tel.: 207-725-3288 *Fax*: 207-725-3083 *Email*: scaref@bowdoin.edu

Information Service   Resources
Bertrand Library
Bucknell University
Lewisburg, Pennsylvania 17837

Bucknell

SPECIAL COLLECTION/UNIVERSITY ARCHIVES

REPRODUCTION OF MATERIALS

It is understood that permission to reproduce materials does not constitute permission to publish. Most copying will be done by library staff as time permits. Factors such as copyright, donor restrictions and physical condition may affect requests for reproduction of Special Collections/University Archives materials. When copying is permitted, the requestor will be asked to sign the "fair use" agreement (see below).

Many published works, unpublished manuscripts, and photographic and audiovisual materials are copyrighted and cannot be reproduced in their entirety without permission of the owner of the intellectual rights to the work. The library frequently does not own the copyright, only the physical item. Persons requesting copies of materials for purposes other than private study must obtain permission from a representative of Information Services and Resources and present written consent of the copyright holder.

FEES (PREPAYMENT REQUIRED)

Photocopying charges for non-profit purposes are $10.00 for the first 20 pages and $.75 for each additional page. Charges for commercial enterprises are $20.00 for the first 20 pages and $1.50 for each additional page.

For non-profit purposes, the digital photographic fee for an 8 1/2" x 11" scan is $22.00. The cost of producing a negative is an additional $11.00. For commercial enterprises, the fee for an 8 1/2" x 11" scan is
        The cost of producing a negative is $22.00.

NOTICE CONCERNING COPYRIGHT RESTRICTIONS

Signature: _____
Date: _____

PHOTOCOPYING POLICY
IRWIN LIBRARY
SPECIAL COLLECTIONS AND RARE BOOKS
UNIVERSITY ARCHIVES

Photocopying can be very destructive to rare books and special collections and university archives materials. Since our goal is to make sure the materials you are using today are still here and in good condition 200 years from now, we need your help in protecting the collections.

Whenever possible, please take notes instead of requesting a photocopy—it will help extend the life of the collections considerably. Also please understand when staff refuses a photocopy request based on the physical condition of an item. Special collections librarians and staff members must walk the fine line between making rare materials accessible now *and* preserving them for future use, so please allow sufficient time in your research to take notes.

Your cooperation is appreciated and helps preserve these materials for future generations of researchers. Thank you for observing the following conditions:

1. The Special Collections and Rare Books area reserves the right to refuse a request for copies if filling the request would result in damage to the materials being copied, or would violate copyright law. Generally, nothing will be copied in its entirety, and no more than 50 pages or one-third of a collection will be copied, whichever is smaller.

2. The library will not make more than one copy of any material, in accordance with the "fair use" provisions of the U.S. Copyright Law (Title 17, U.S. Code).

3. All photocopying is done for researchers by Special Collections and Rare Books staff. Requests will be filled as quickly as possible, based on staff time and photocopier access. If necessary, you may be asked to pick up your copies the next day, or have them mailed to you.

4. Copies are made for private study, scholarship, or research use only. Except for "fair use," they may not be reproduced or published in any fashion without prior permission from the copyright holder.

PHOTOCOPYING FEE SCHEDULE

As of July 15, 2000, fees for photocopying per page are:

For Butler students, faculty, staff: 10 cents

For researchers unaffiliated with Butler: 25 cents

Butler University

PHOTOCOPY REQUEST FORM
Special Collections and Rare Books
Butler University Libraries

Name:_____Status:_____

Address:_____

City, State, Zip:_____ Phone:_____

PHOTOCOPYING POLICY
1. The Special Collections and Rare Books area reserves the right to refuse a request for copies if filling the request would result in damage to the materials being copied, or would violate copyright law. Generally, nothing will be copied in its entirety, and no more than 50 pages or one-third of a collection will be copied, whichever is smaller.
2. The library will not make more than one copy of any material, in accordance with the "fair use" provisions of the U.S. Copyright Law (Title 17, U.S. Code).
3. All photocopying is done for researchers by Special Collections and Rare Books staff. Requests will be filled as quickly as possible, based on staff time and photocopier access. If necessary, you may be asked to pick up your copies the next day, or have them mailed to you.
4. Copies are made for private study, scholarship, or research use only. Except for "fair use," they may not be reproduced or published in any fashion without prior permission from the copyright holder.

WARNING CONCERNING COPYRIGHT RESTRICTIONS

The copyright law of the United States (Title 17, United States Code) governs the making of photocopies or other reproductions of copyrighted material. Under certain conditions specified in the law, libraries and archives are authorized to furnish a photocopy or other reproduction. One of these specified conditions is that the photocopy or reproduction is not to be used for any purpose other than private study, scholarship, or research. If a researcher makes a request for, or later uses a photocopy or reproduction for purposes in excess of this "fair use," that researcher may be liable for copyright infringement. This institution reserves the right to refuse a request for photocopying if, in the judgement of the professional staff, filling the request would violate copyright law.

I have read the above information and warning and understand that written permission must be obtained from the copyright holder prior to publication of photocopied material. I assume full legal responsibility for any infringement of copyright that might occur from the use or publication of this material through my failure to obtain appropriate permissions.

The photocopies ordered will be used only for the following purpose:_____

Signature:_____ Date:_____

Please place requests on back of form.

Title/Collection Name:_____

Call Number:_____ Vol. No._____

Box/Folder Number:_____

Pages or dates:_____

_____

Title/Collection Name:_____

Call Number:_____ Vol. No._____

Box/Folder Number:_____

Pages or dates:_____

_____

Title/Collection Name:_____

Call Number:_____ Vol. No._____

Box/Folder Number:_____

Pages or dates:_____

_____

Title/Collection Name:_____

Call Number:_____ Vol. No._____

Box/Folder Number:_____

Pages or dates:_____

_____

Title/Collection Name:_____

Call Number:_____ Vol. No._____

Box/Folder Number:_____

Pages or dates:_____

_____

PHOTOCOPY ORDER FORM
HONNOLD/MUDD LIBRARY -SPECIAL COLLECTIONS

The Claremont Colleges

I agree to use this material for study and research purposes only, and not for publication.

DATE _____CALL NO._____

SIGNATURE _____

FOR (PLEASE PRINT NAME) _____

ADDRESS (IF SENT) _____

PHONE (PICK-UP) _____ ORDER TAKEN BY_____

WARNING: The photocopies you request may be Protected by copyright law (Title 17 U.S.Code)

PHOTOCOPY PAGES:

TOTAL NO. OF SHEETS _____

TOTAL COST _____   PAID_____

CHARGES:
Patron pick-up: 25 cents per sheet
Order mailed: 35 cents per sheet ($3.00 minimum) Prepayment is required on all orders over $20.00

Make checks payable to:
Honnold/Mudd Library

Mailing address:
Honnold/Mudd Library
Special Collections
800 N. Dartmouth Avenue
Claremont, CA 91711-3991

Scanning Order Form
Honnold/Mudd Library – Special Collections

Name (please print)_____
I agree to use this material for study and research purposes only, and not for publication.

Signature _____Date_____

Title/Call No. _____

Address (if sent) _____

Phone/Email (pick-up) _____Order Taken _____

Warning: The scanning you request may be protected by Copyright Law (Title 17 U.S. Code).
Special Collections reserves the right to refuse to scan large, fragile, and/or brittle material and any material sensitive to light. All orders are subject to approval by Special Collections staff. Three working days advance notice is required for all scanning orders.

Scan Pages:

Resolution (dpi/ppi):_____ In: B&W / Color

File Format (tiff, jpeg, gif, etc.): _____

Total # of images: _____

Total cost: _____ Paid _____

Charges: Small Orders: $5.00 per image
Large Orders*: $40.00 per hour
CDs: $1 each CD-R
*Large orders are generally those that require an hour or more to accomplish, either due to the volume or complexity of the order.

Make Checks payable to: Honnold/Mudd Library

Mailing Address: Honnold/Mudd Library
Special Collections

© The Libraries of the Claremont Colleges

Davidson College

Davidson College Archives
E. H. Little Library
P.O. Box 7200
Davidson, NC 28035-7200

APPLICATION FOR PERMISSION TO REPRODUCE PHOTOGRAPHS

Name of Applicant:_____

Organization or Agency (if appropriate):_____

Address:_____

MATERIAL TO BE REPRODUCED
Title or description of item:

INTENDED USE OF MATERIAL

CONDITIONS OF USE:

1. All requests to reproduce items from our holdings must be submitted on this application. By signing this application, the applicant agrees to abide by all conditions and provisions.

Permission for reproduction is granted only when this application is countersigned by an authorized representative of the repository. Permission for reproduction is limited to the applicant and is non-transferable.

Permission for reproduction is granted only for the purpose described in this application. This permission is non-exclusive; the repository reserves the right to reproduce the image and to allow others to reproduce the image.

Any subsequent use (including subsequent editions, paperback editions, foreign language editions, electronic editions, etc.) constitutes reuse and must be applied for in writing to the repository.

The repository reserves the right to refuse reproduction of its holdings if it feels fulfillment of that order would be in violation of copyright law or other law. The repository reserves the right to refuse reproduction of its holdings and to impose such conditions as it may deem advisable in the best interests of the repository.

2. In addition to the permission of the repository, additional permission may be required. Those permissions may include, but are not limited to:

COPYRIGHT: The Davidson College Archives does not hold the copyright to all items in its collection. If the work is subject to copyright, the copyright remains with the producer or publisher of the work or others to whom the copyright may have been assigned. The researcher is responsible for obtaining permission from the copyright holder before publishing any of this material.

PRIVACY: An individual depicted in a reproduction has privacy rights as outlined in "Protection of Human Subjects," Title 45 *Code of Federal Regulations*, Pt. 46. The repository reserves the right to require a release from individuals whose privacy may be violated by the publication of an image.

3. All reproductions should include the credit line "Courtesy of the Davidson College Archives."

4. Images may be cropped to suit design and layout, but they may not be altered for drawn upon or manipulated in any way so that they look different from the way they appear in the historical collection.

5. The applicant agrees to pay the reproduction fees assigned. Photographs: 8x10 Black and white-$10.00; 8x10 Color $12.00; 5x7 Black and White $7.50; 5x7 Color $9.00.

By signing this application, I accept personally and on behalf of any organization I represent the conditions set forth above:

Signed:_____   Date:_____

When signed by an authorized agent of the repository, this form constitutes permission for reproduction as outlined in this application.

Signed:_____   Date:_____

Lafayette College

LAFAYETTE COLLEGE

David Bishop Skillman Library

SPECIAL COLLECTIONS AND ARCHIVES

REQUEST FOR PHOTOGRAPHIC REPRODUCTION

Name _____

Address_____

City _____ State _____ Zip _____

Material to be Reproduced

Collection _____

Item *(brief identifying description)*   Location *(box/folder)*

Intended Use of Copies _____

_____

(continued on back)

92 Reprographics Policies and Related Forms

Easton, Pennsylvania 18042-1797   •   Telephone 610-330-5151

The Lafayette College Special Collections and Archives provides for photographic reproduction of the above materials under the following conditions:

1. Reproductions are provided under the doctrine of fair use and are governed under the United States Copyright Act (Title 17, U.S. Code). See the Notice below. The researcher is liable for any infringement of the provisions of this Act.

2. Reproduction of archival or manuscript materials does not constitute permission to publish from those materials. Permission to publish any materials in their entirety or a substantial portion thereof must be obtained in writing prior to publication from the Lafayette College Special Collections and Archives. It is the sole responsibility of the researcher to request this permission.

3. The researcher agrees to hold harmless the Lafayette College Special Collections and Archives and its staff against all claims and actions arising out of his/her use of the materials.

Signature _____ Date _____

NOTICE
WARNING CONCERNING COPYRIGHT
RESTRICTIONS

The copyright law of the United States (Title 17, United States Code) governs the making of photocopies or other reproductions of copyrighted material.

Under certain conditions specified in the law, libraries and archives are authorized to furnish a photocopy or other reproduction. One of these specified conditions is that the photocopy or reproduction is not to be "used for any purpose other than private study, scholarship, or research." If a user makes a request for, or later uses, a photocopy or reproduction for purposes in excess of "fair use," that user may be liable for copyright infringement.

The institution reserves the right to refuse to accept a copying order if, in its judgment, fulfillment of the order would involve a violation of copyright law.

Photographic Use Form

Photographic copies in any format are provided by the North Central College Archives for use with the following understandings:

1. Any use of the image or copy will be accompanied by a credit line "Courtesy of North Central College Archives".
2. Permission is granted only for the stated purpose below. The North Central College Archives should be contacted regarding any subsequent use.
3. The user assumes responsibility for conforming to the laws of libel, privacy, and copyright.
4. Copies are not to be deposited in any other library or repository.

Description of Photograph: _____

Intended Use: _____

_____

_____

Publication Title or Web site (if applicable): _____

Name: _____

Affiliation: _____

Address: _____

Phone: _____ E-mail: _____

Signature: _____

Date: _____

cas/kjb
9/04

South Caroliniana Library – Digital Reproduction
Please read and sign the following before completing Side 2.

(Please print)

NAME_____ DATE_____

ADDRESS_____   PLEASE MAIL   Y

_____   WILL PICK UP IN OFFICE   Y

TELEPHONE _____(For use **ONLY** if there is a problem with the order.)

CONDITIONS

1. PAYMENT REQUIRED IN ADVANCE. Copies can usually be made in 1 – 2 weeks. Staff constraints make it impossible to call patrons when their orders are ready

2. Personal scanners and digital cameras are NOT allowed. Scanning is handled by the Library staff because of the age, condition, and rarity of most of our collections. The Library reserves the right to limit or refuse reproduction of items such as bound newspapers and any other materials that may be damaged in the process. Photographs will be scanned ONLY if there is a surrogate copy available. Traditional photographic reproductions still produce much higher-quality copies than do scanned images. CD burning is not available.

3. All responsibility for questions of copyright and literary rights that may arise in this copying and in the use made of the copies is assumed by the applicant. Copyright materials will not be reproduced beyond recognized "fair use" without the signed authorization of the copyright owner. Special permission for reprinting, reproducing, or extensive quotation from rare books or manuscripts must be obtained through written application to the Director, stating the use to be made of the material.

4. The Library does not sell copies, but merely performs the service of copying. The fee paid is exclusively for such service. Scanning prices are higher than those for photocopies due to its labor-intensive process. The Library reserves the right to recall all scanned copies within a stipulated time. The Library reserves the right, at its discretion and without explanation: to limit the number of copies; to restrict the use or further reproduction of rare or valuable material; to make special quotations on material involving unusual difficulty. Digital reproduction orders must be signed by a Library staff member before copies can be provided.

NOTICE RE COPYRIGHT RESTRICTIONS

The copyright law of the United States (Title 17, United States Code) governs the making of photocopies or other reproductions of copyright materials. Under certain conditions specified by law, libraries and archives are authorized to furnish a photocopy or other reproduction. One of the specific conditions is that the photocopy or reproduction is not to be "used for any purpose other than private study, scholarship, or research." If a user makes a request for, or later uses, a photocopy or reproduction in excess of "fair use," that user may be liable for copyright infringement. This institution reserves the right to refuse to accept a copy order if, in its judgement, fulfillment of the order would involve violation of copyright law.

By signing this form, the patron agrees: 1) not to remove or crop the embedded credit line in each digital image, 2) not to duplicate or manipulate the digital image, as any such action constitutes copyright violation, 3) not to use the image for any additional purposes other than those specified on this form, unless additional permission is obtained from the Library director.

I hereby agree to the above conditions: _____

                                       (Patron signature)

                                       Staff Initials_____

University of South Carolina

CHARGES

An initial flat fee of $5.00 applies to each order, with an additional charges:

Bond paper (print size up to 8 ½ x 14")..$.50 per sheet
Photo-quality paper ....$3.00 per sheet
Scan to disk (patrons must provide new, empty disks)....................$10.00 per image

Postage/handling fees

Orders on bond paper: use .50 photocopy order chart
Orders on photo-quality paper: 1-3 pages - $2 flat fee; 4-10 pages - $5 flat fee; over 10 pages - $10 flat fee
Orders on disk:
　　NOTE: A use fee may also apply if items are to be published. This includes the internet.

DESCRIPTION OF MATERIALS (Specify number of pages per item, and if the title page is to be copied):

_____
_____
_____
_____
_____
_____
_____
_____
_____
_____
_____
_____
_____
_____
_____
_____
_____
_____
_____
_____
_____
_____

For SCL Use Only		
CHARGES No. of copies_____	PRODUCTION OF COPIES Operator Initials_____	DELIVERY OF COPIES Staff Initials_____
Total Charges_____ Y Prepaid　　Y No charge	Date _____	Date_____

University of Wisconsin-Green Bay

Special Collections Policies

PHOTOCOPYING AND PROCESSING FEES

Self-service Copying

$.10 per image for paper records; $.25 per image for microfilm and microfiche records

Self-service Scanning

Scan to laser printer: $1.00 per image

Scan to disk/CD: $1.00 per image + $2.50 disk/CD fee

Scan to e-mail: no charge

Copying Services

A $5.00 advance payment will be required for each name searched in each of these types of records: Vital records (birth, marriage, death); citizenship records; census records; court records; probate records; tax rolls; other public records; manuscript collections and published sources (books, maps).

If the record requested is found and is less than 5 pages in length, a copy will be provided at no additional charge. If the record is found and is more than 5 pages in length, a cost estimate will be provided using the following guidlines:

$.50 per page for copies from paper records
$.60 per page for copies from microfilm records

If you would like us to proceed with the copy job after you have received our cost estimate, you must pay that amount in advance.

Search & Copy Request Forms for the various types of records are available on-line to print, fill out, and mail in with your check. At this time, we are unable to accept credit card payments, online, or phone requests.

Photographic Prints

When ordering media reproductions, please include identification numbers, any published references, and photocopies of the images. Also, please state the intended use of the materials requested. Any special copying, handling or mailing instructions should be included with the order. Negatives are not provided for photographic orders. All fees are subject to change. All sales are final. Some material may not be available for copying due to restrictions. All responsibility for questions of copyright that may arise in copying and in the use of copies will be assumed by the user. A signed Indemnification Agreement is required for all publication and production use.

If a negative is on file:

> 4 x 5 - $5.00
> 5 x 7 - $7.50
> 8 x 10 - $7.50

If a negative is NOT on file:

> 4 x 5 - $7.50
> 5 x 7 - $10.00
> 8 x 10 - $12.50

Prices for other sizes available upon request. Each reproduction job will also have a $5.00 processing charge. Normal delivery time is 2 weeks.

Oral History Recordings

All reproductions are produced on audio cassettes. If the original is on a reel-to-reel tape there is a $8.00 set up fee. Fees are based on number of minutes copied:

> 0-30 minutes - $7.50
>
> 30-60 minutes - $8.00
>
> 60-90 minutes - $9.00

All responsibility for questions of copyright that may arise in copying and in the use of copies will be assumed by the user. A signed Indemnification Agreement is required for all publication and production use.

Each reproduction job will also have a $15.00 processing charge. Normal delivery time is 2 weeks.

Scanning

Many of the materials in the Special Collections Department can be scanned. All responsibility for questions of copyright that may arise in scanning and in the use of copies will be assumed by the user. A signed Indemnification Agreement is required for all publication and production use.

Scan to laser printer - $1.00 per image
Scan to disk/CD - $1.00 per image and $2.50 disk/CD fee

Scan to e-mail: $1.00 per image.

Each scanning job will also have a $15.00 processing charge. Normal delivery time is 2 weeks.

Other Media

Charges for reproductions of videos, film, and filmstrips are available upon request. Architectural drawings are $5.00 each.

Notarizing

There will be a $5.00 handling fee for notarizing of documents.

All responsibility for questions of copyright that may arise in copying and in the use of copies will be assumed by the user. A signed Indemnification Agreement is required for all publication and production use.

COLLECTION DEVELOPMENT POLICES

Abell Library Special Collections
Austin College
Collection Development Policy

Purpose

The Special Collections of Abell Library supports the teaching and research needs of the Austin College community and also serves as a repository for precious artifacts that would otherwise be unavailable to the local public.[1] The goal of Special Collections is to establish and maintain special collections of materials which are distinctive to the region, provide archival support to the College, or fulfill the obligation of the Library to preserve rare and special materials. To these ends, Special Collections actively collects library and archival materials relating to the historical and cultural development of Austin College and the American Southwest, especially Texas. The collecting areas discussed in this policy are: the Rare Books Collection, Special Collections, and College Archives.

As artifacts, objects in special collections are of interest either because they contain information inscribed upon them, or present information in themselves (whether associatively, through provenance, or inherently, as in the way a hand press book has been printed and assembled.) Artifactual information includes texts and illustrations. The artifacts in Special Collections, therefore, can have at least three values: They provide information about their texts, or they provide information about publishing, reading, ownership and all that we call the history of the book, or they are aesthetically appealing. The range of aesthetic values can be considerable. Some books have particularly appealing bindings such as hand-tooled leather or gold leaf. Some books are a pleasure to hold and to read, such as Aldine octavos or Modern Library editions. The books most celebrated as beautiful are typically those which add extraordinary design to important textual content, such as the *Book of Kells* and the Cranston and Curts illustrated Bible. But the primary value of books as artifacts is the way in which they provide information about their texts, both explicitly and implicitly. Readers come to the library to find information in books, and less often (though importantly) to study the book as object to gain further information about the text or about history more broadly considered. The artifacts, beyond the texts, provide information on the history of the book as a socially-created and socially-consumed object. The physical design and construction of the book provides evidence as to the way readers were intended to perceive it. Often, too, individual books themselves will have a history, and become evidence of the transmission of ideas.[2] In the electronic age, special collections will continue in importance because of the continuing importance of artifactual documents.[3] Therefore, Austin College recognizes the importance of preserving such artifacts in its possession.

In general, in kind gifts of "special collections" to Abell Library must fall within one of the three broad collecting areas and be further judged within the collecting scope of that particular area. While all donations may be permanently identified as to provenance (donor), only those items meeting the selection criteria of Special

Collections will be physically housed in Special Collections and will then become a part of that collecting area.

Rare Books Collection

The Rare Books Collection at Austin College is comprised of four major categories: The Julio Berzunza Collection on Alexander the Great; modern European history, literature and culture (primarily the British Isles); nineteenth century periodicals; and religion and theology (emphasis on the Reformation). Languages represented include all the Romance languages, Greek, Hebrew, Chaldean, English, German, Scandinavian, and American Indian.

General Guidelines - Materials in the Rare Books Collection are acquired through donation or transfer from the general stacks. Items are judged on the basis of rarity (e.g. early printing; limited edition; valuable autograph or inscripton; fine binding; high market value of comparable item); fine plates or illustrations which could be easily removed or stolen; physical fragility when preservation is necessary and the item cannot be rebound; or upon expert recommendation. They are non-circulating and in closed stacks but may be used by library patrons during Reading Room hours with the assistance of library staff.

Nineteenth Century Periodicals

The Nineteenth Century Periodicals Collection was established in 1995 in order to preserve and secure original issues of nineteenth century periodicals within Abell Library. Most titles are American periodicals although a few English and one French publication are represented. Some early (pre-1920s) twentieth century volumes are included because of their physical condition. Although almost all volumes are bound, the collection contains some issues in their original unbound state. Special Collections does not actively seek additions to this collection beyond the titles in the Library's existing holdings except for Texas imprints.

Modern European History, Literature and Culture

The core of this collection was a gift from Dr. Virginia Irvine Blocker, wife of Dr. Truman G. Blocker, Austin College alumnus and trustee. The Irvine Collection, established in 1978, consists of the personal library of Mrs. Annie Irvine, formerly associate professor of English at the University of Texas at Austin. Outstanding volumes include complete first and second editions of Holinshed's *Chronicles of England.* Other books in the collection, including a facsimile of the *Book of Kells* and a collection of first editions by William Butler Yeats, were either purchased for the library, or donated by other benefactors throughout the history of the College. The oldest volume is a 1567 Venetian imprint. English is the primary language of the collection; however, this includes both Middle and Modern English. Other languages represented are Latin,

French, Spanish, and Italian. Special Collections does not actively seek additions to this collection outside the Library's existing holdings.

Religion and Theology

Books in this category pertain exclusively to modern Christianity, spanning the period from the sixteenth through early twentieth centuries. Topics include church history, missionary history, biography, theological treatises, church canon, prayer books, Bibles and biblical scholarship, sermons, homilies, and sacred music. This collection of bound volumes was gradually acquired through gifts and purchases over the history of the College, the first books having been acquired in 1850. A number of volumes belonged to early presidents of Austin College. The two largest in kind gifts were the libraries of Reverend Jerome Twitchell, an early trustee, in 1857, and Dr. Thomas Stone Clyce, President 1900-1932, circa 1946. English and Latin are primary languages of the collection. Greek, Hebrew, Chaldean, German, Swedish, Finnish, and several American Indian languages are also represented. The Special Collections Division does not actively seek additions to this collection outside the Library's existing holdings.

The Julio Berzunza Collection of Alexander the Great

The Julio Berzunza Alexander the Great Collection consists of books, pamphlets, periodicals, maps, engravings, and artifacts totaling nearly 1,000 items relating to the life of Alexander the Great, compiled between 1922 and 1959. Dates of material range from late fifteenth through mid-twentieth century, the earliest volume being 1478. The collection was purchased in 1959 from the estate of Julio Berzunza, a professor of Romance Languages at the University of New Hampshire, and contains many items that are extremely rare. Latin is the primary language in the collection. French, Spanish, Italian, German, English, Greek and Oriental languages are also represented. Special Collections does not seek additions to this collection.

Other Special Collections

General Guidelines - Materials are added to Special Collections through donation or transfer from the general stacks. Gifts must fall within the active collecting scope outlined in the Special Collections statement of purpose, i.e. the American Southwest and Austin College. Moreover, items selected for inclusion in Special Collections at Austin College must, in and of themselves, be unique or valuable to the institution in some way, either associatively or intrinsically. Special Collections material is non-circulating[*] and in closed stacks but may be used by library patrons during Rare Books Room hours with the assistance of library staff. Some material, not duplicated in the general stacks, may be available to faculty for limited check-out by special arrangement with the Archivist and Head of Circulation.

---

[*] With the exception of some portions of the Texas and Southwest Collection. See specific policies for the Texas and Southwest Collection.

Austin College recognizes that all libraries have books and documents that acquire significant cultural, historical, and/or financial value over time and that such books need to be protected. Criteria for selective identification of such material include age, intrinsic characteristics and qualities (e.g. special bindings, extra-illustrated volumes, significant provenance, decorated endpapers, fine printing, unusual paper, portfolios, valuable maps, plates, or printed ephemera, local authorship, unusual formats, or difficulty of replacement), condition (e.g. late nineteenth and early twentieth century volumes that cannot be repaired or rebound, including dustjackets), and bibliographical, research, or market value.[4] As a custodial function, Special Collections brings together all books and materials in need of conservation and protection because of their fragility, format, or intrinsic value. These materials may not be actively sought, but when they are received by the Library or identified within its existing collections, they should be transferred to Special Collections. These materials include:

a. Early Imprints. These are identified as works printed **before**:

1. 1880 in England, continental Europe, and the United States east of the Mississippi River, in South America, in Central America, and in Canada;

2. 1901 in the United States west of the Mississippi River;

3. 1926 in Africa, Asia, and the Pacific.

b. Materials with Unusual Bibliographic Characteristics. These may include:

1. Editions limited to 500 copies or less;

2. Significant first editions;

3. Association or autograph copies, when significant;

4. Extra-illustrated or grangerized books;

5. Works distinguished by illustrations, typography, binding, fore-edge painting, or the like.

c. Materials with Unusual Physical Characteristics. These include:

1. Materials in unusual formats, e.g. broadsides, ephemera, playbills, portfolios, prints;

2. Materials of unusual size, e.g. large folios and miniatures;

The Pate Texana Collection

The Pate Texana Collection was given to the Austin College Library by Dr. and Mrs. Adlai McMillan Pate, Jr. in 1975 and was added to by the donors periodically until Dr. Pate's death in 1989. In addition to books, the collection contains pamphlets, newspaper, periodicals, broadsides, maps, manuscripts, artwork and ephemera related to Texas history, literature, and culture from the early nineteenth century to the late twentieth century. The collection was originally built around the figure of Sam Houston, one of the founders of Austin College in 1849 and a member of its board of trustees until his death in 1863. While it is especially rich in materials relating to Sam Houston, it is also outstanding for its number of county histories. Its greatest strength, however, is its broad coverage of all periods of Texas history, making it especially suitable for an under-graduate library.

The Rex and Mary Strickland Southwestern Collection

The Rex and Mary Strickland Southwestern Collection was given to Austin College in January of 1984, and represents Dr. Strickland's professional library. Dr. Rex Strickland graduated from Austin College in 1936. He was a well-known Texas historian who taught for many years at the University of Texas at El Paso. The Strickland Southwestern Collection includes books, pamphlets, manuscripts, broadsides, artworks and ephemera relating to Texas and the Southwest. The strength of the collection is its coverage of west Texas and the desert Southwest. It is particularly rich in the artwork of Texas illustrators Tom Lea and José Cisneros, and the printing of Carl Hertzog. Language of the collection is English. The Southwestern Collection originally comprised one third of the Rex and Mary Strickland library, which also included European, ancient and miscellaneous histories, United States history and Americana. Most of these materials remain in the library's main collection, identified as to provenance.

The Margaret White Hoard Collection

The Hoard Collection, donated to Austin College in the 1950s, was the College's first Texana collection. In addition to her library, Mrs. Hoard gave a check to the college annually for many years for the purchase of additional Texas books for her collection. Mrs. Hoard was a member of one of the founding families of Whitewright, Texas, and her husband was an Austin College alumnus and prominent local businessman. The collection contains bound volumes covering all periods of Texas history. Its particular strengths are county histories and Texas folklore. English is the predominant language of the collection.

The Lewis F. Russell Collection

The Lewis F. Russell Collection was donated to Austin College in late 1997. Judge Russell was a member of the Dallas, Texas, bench and bar for many years. His son

3. Other unusual characteristics, such as fragile or delicate bindings, boxes which should be preserved, or awkward shapes.

d. Materials Especially Prone to Loss, Damage, or Mutilation. These include:

1. Volumes of fine, loose, or tipped-in plates;

2. Volumes with manuscript materials laid or tipped-in;

3. Volumes with bound or laid-in material, such as maps, subject to mutilation;

4. Erotica;

5. Other out-of-print or physically fragile materials when preservation is necessary and the item cannot be rebound, and items identified by faculty or other expert as requiring special protection.

In addition to books transferred from the general collection because they meet one or more of the above criteria, Special Collections consists of three other major collecting areas: Texas and Southwest Studies, the Autographed Collection, and the J. Gilbert E. Wright Collection of literature on spiritualism, parapsychology, and the occult.

Texas and Southwest Studies Collection

General Guidelines - Materials in the Texas and Southwest Studies Collection are added through purchase, donation, and transfer from the general stacks. Selected items from four major donations form the core of the collection: The Pate Texana Collection, The Margaret White Hoard Collection, The Rex and Mary Strickland Southwestern Collection, and the Lewis F. Russell Collection. These collections are complemented by books purchased through a grant from the Erwin E. Smith Foundation. The Texas and Southwest Studies Collection contains books, pamphlets, periodicals, maps, broadsides, manuscripts, artworks, historical artifacts, and ephemera relating to the history, literature, and culture of the American Southwest. The primary collecting focus, however, is books. The primary language of the collection is English, but Spanish, French, and German language imprints are also represented.

Some books in the Texas and Southwest Collection may be checked out by Austin College students and faculty. However, they are not available for interlibrary loan. Books in the collection are also subject to the same selection criteria for protection and preservation set out in the General Guidelines for Special Collections. A book may, therefore, be withdrawn from circulation if necessary. Although Austin College actively seeks to purchase books on Texas and the Southwest, because such purchases are intended primarily for circulation, the college seeks copies that do not have added value such as dust jackets, signatures, inscriptions, and significant first or limited editions.

"Lucky" is an alumnus of Austin College. The Russell collection contains many pristine first editions still in original dustjackets and slipcases, maps, pamphlets, and ephemera. Its greatest contributions to the Texas and Southwest Studies Collection, however, are its many volumes of Texas fiction, post-1950 imprints, town histories, and biographies. English is the predominant language of the collection. Also included in the Russell Collection are law books and miscellaneous Americana. Most of these materials have been incorporated into the library's main collection, identified as to provenance.

Autographed Collection

The Autographed Collection was established in 1996 by Library Director, Dr. Larry Hardesty, to celebrate the activities and achievements of the Austin College community. Additions are made through purchase, donations, and transfer from the general collection. Special Collections actively collects materials published by Austin College faculty, students, alumni, and friends of the College, inscribed and/or signed by their authors. Whenever possible within budget limitations, duplicate copies of autographed books should be obtained for general stacks. English is the primary language of the material in the Autographed Collection. However Japanese and Spanish are also represented. Because of the multi-cultural nature of the pool of contributors, there are no language restrictions on items acquired for this collection.

J. Gilbert E. Wright Collection

The J. Gilbert E. Wright Collection was donated to Arthur Hopkins Library at Austin College in 1961 by his son and daughter-in-law, L. M. (Pat) Wright and Patricia Hopkins Wright. As a research chemist, Wright developed an interest in the "borderland" sciences and psychic research, and he became correspondent with such notables in the field as Conan Doyle, Charles Richet, and Prince Youreavitch. His collection contains books relating to spiritualism, parapsychology, and the occult, published between 1850 and the late 1950s. The primary language of the collection is English though French and German are also represented. The college does not actively seek to add to this collection. These materials have been incorporated into the library's main collection, identified as to provenance

College Archives

Special Collections serves as the archival repository for Austin College. As such, the division acquires college records that are judged by the archivist to have enduring historical value. Emphasis is placed on collecting the records of key policy-makers at the college, such as the President and Vice President of Academic Affairs. The college material is primarily archival in nature and includes correspondence, memoranda, financial and statistical reports, budgets, minutes, photographs and negatives, slides, films, oral history interviews, plans, proposals, scrapbooks, and computer generated records. Printed material such as university publications, newspapers and newsletters, yearbooks, and university catalogs are also collected. Except for special exhibits and displays, artifacts are not actively solicited.

---

[1] Printed material, manuscripts, and, in some instances, artwork. The chief example of such precious artifacts is the *Book of Kells*. Others include the *Holinshed Chronicles* and incunabula found in the Berzunza collection, which many local residents would never have the opportunity to experience were it not for the college preserving them.

[2] i.e. this book was made in this place at this time, has this reader's name in it, has these marks in it, and was found in this place at this later time, etc.

[3] Peter S. Graham, "New Roles for Special Collections on the Network," as submitted to *College & Research Libraries*, February, 1998; reported publication date May, 1998.

[4] ACRL Standards for the Selection of Materials for Transfer to Special Collections 2d edition (1994).

Bowdoin College Archives & Records Management Collection Policy
[*rev. 02072001*]

This policy is based on the Bowdoin College Archives Records Authority Statement, approved by the Executive Committee of the Governing Boards, June 10, 1994.

Selection:

The Bowdoin College Archives acquires, preserves, maintains, and provides access to those College records that possess enduring administrative, legal, fiscal, or historical value. The purpose for collecting such records is to provide a complete institutional record of the College and to document its activities, particularly: its history; its functions of teaching, learning and research; its socializing aspects; its role in the community (especially as a cultural agent); and, its place in American higher education.

The decision to preserve College records for administrative, legal and fiscal purposes is the responsibility of the appropriate College officer or administrator in consultation with the College Archives. The decision to acquire records of historic value is the responsibility of the College Archives.

The Archives welcomes offers of privately owned materials that bear on the history of the College and on the experiences of the College community. Faculty papers, letters and reminiscences of alumni/ae, reunion keepsakes, photographs, and related documents supplement and fortify the official College record, and the Archives is happy to receive such acquisitions provided their acceptance incurs no obligation to retain such material as a distinct collection or in any prescribed physical form.

Ownership and Retention:

All College records are the property of Bowdoin College and are subject to records retention schedules, which are determined by the officer in charge of the accumulated records in consultation with the College Archives. Retention periods and ultimate disposition for these records are based on legal, administrative and institutional considerations. None of these records may be destroyed or otherwise disposed of without the approval of both the official record holder and the College Archives. ["Records Authority Statement" (Exec.Comm. of the Governing Boards of Bowdoin College, June 10, 1994)]

All College records must be retained in a readable format. While records are in the custody of the office of origin, all requirements associated with records retention, such as maintenance of filing systems, storage and access, remain the responsibility of the official record holder. Records scheduled for permanent retention shall be managed in accordance with campus-wide practices and procedures under the direction of the College Archives and, with respect to electronic records, of Computing & Information Services [CIS]. Responsibility to read, to retrieve and to preserve information from inactive and Archival electronic records rests with the office of origin.

All College records preserved in the Archives remain the records of the office of origin and may be withdrawn at any time by that office for its own use. In the absence of specified restrictions, all records retained in the Archives will be available for research following the established guidelines of Special Collections & Archives.

Copyright in College records may rest with Bowdoin College or, in some cases, with the author of the work. Published use of College records beyond "fair use" as stipulated in U.S. copyright law (Title 17 *U.S.Code*) requires the express written permission of the copyright holder. Please consult the Bowdoin College Copyright Policy or Special Collections & Archives staff for further information.

Definitions:

College record: all recorded information and data, regardless of physical form or characteristics, that are created or received in the course of official College business and that document the administrative transactions and activities of any College office or employee, including those by or with teaching faculty and students in the performance of their official administrative College obligations, constitute College records and are the property of Bowdoin College. Examples include: official correspondence; committee minutes and reports; transcripts; grade books; student coursework and examinations; financial data; personnel and search committee files; College publications; recordings of official College events; policies; email and voicemail communications related to College business.

Personal record: all recorded information and data that are created or received independent of official administrative College business constitute personal records and are the property of the holder of those materials or data. Examples include: teaching materials; scholarly research; unsanctioned student publications; recordings of informal events; email and voicemail unrelated to College business.

Mixed records: recorded information and data that co-mingle "College records" with either personal records or official records of another institution or agency require defined custody to establish whether or not Bowdoin College shall claim stewardship over such mixed records. In any event, those portions of the mixed records that meet the definition of "College records" are subject to the information policies of Bowdoin College. Examples include: collaborative projects involving Bowdoin faculty and College administrative units; CBB consortial ventures.

Active records: records required for the ongoing business activities of the record holder; these records carry the potential for frequent and timely consultation.

Inactive records: records of administrative value but not essential to the ongoing business activities of the record holder; these records may carry auditing, legal or other stipulations that require their retention but only occasional consultation.

Archival records: records of enduring value to the College that are designated for permanent retention once their active or inactive cycle has passed. Archival records in most physical forms, including paper-based texts, photographs and magnetic media, are normally transferred to the custody of the College Archives for storage, preservation, access, and retrieval. Some electronic records may be designated as "Archival" and in the custodial control of the College Archives but may reside on storage devices outside the physical confines of College Archives facilities.

Copy of record: sometimes thought of as the "master copy," a single copy of a document maintained by its office of origin or designated custodian that is designated as the official College record of a transaction or activity; all other copies are duplicate copies, held for convenience, and should be destroyed in the specified manner as soon as their usefulness has ended.

Office of origin: department, administrative unit or designated College officer responsible for the creation or ongoing custody of a College "copy of record" prior to its scheduled destruction or transfer to the Archives.

Records retention schedules: documents created by the Archives, in consultation with the appropriate College officer(s), that define particular groups of College records, indicate when those records become inactive, specify whether or not they should be transferred to the Archives for temporary or permanent storage and whether they are subject to general or confidential destruction, and stipulate what access restrictions apply to their use.

Canisius College

SPECIAL COLLECTIONS

COLLECTION DEVELOPMENT POLICY

General Purpose

The purpose of Special Collections is to preserve in good condition and to display the most valuable or unique items in the library. The collections is set apart from the main library collection not necessarily to restrict access to these materials but rather to monitor their physical condition and to call attention to rare and unusual items that the library owns.

General Subject Boundaries

Material to be included in Special Collections should fit into one or more of the following categories:

-Jesuitica

-early printed tracts (medieval to nineteenth century) on theology or philosophy

-early manuscripts (up to and including the sixteenth century)

-books autographed by a well-known author

-Charles A. Brady materials

-Irish literature

-works on early Buffalo history

-materials relating to the history of the Canisius College Library

-books, manuscripts, and other materials that can be proven to be unique or rare or are of interest to Canisius College

Religious materials, specifically those having to do with Roman Catholicism, dominate the subject scope of the collection. Special Collections does not collect material having to do with the history of Canisius College as that is the purpose of the sep arate Archives unit on campus.

Size of Collection

Special Collections contains approximately 2000 items, 1000 of which are master's theses produced by students obtaining degrees from Canisius College. Ten manuscripts (handwritten works) are included in the collection.

Languages

The predominant languages of Special Collections material are English and Latin. Some Greek works are also included as are a couple of Arabic works.

Chronological Coverage

Materials in Special Collections date from the fifteenth century to the present day.

Geographical Coverage

Most materials in Special Collections are of European or American origin.

Format and Type of Materials Collected

Special Collections is a print collection. It includes both manuscripts written on vellum and books printed on paper.

Other Local Resources Available

Buffalo is home to a number of fine historical collections of printed material, most notably the Buffalo and Erie County Historical Society, the Rare Book Department of the Buffalo and Erie County Public Library, and the Poetry and Rare Book Collec tion of the State University of New York at Buffalo. In addition, St. Bonaventure University maintains an outstanding collection of early religious works and also houses the Franciscan Institute, and other college libraries such as Niagara University main tain rare books collections locally.

Special Considerations

The Canisius College Library does not actively engage in building Special Collections by purchase of highly valuable or unique items. Neither is there a budget line devoted to such purchases. Instead, most material makes its way into the collection through donation or transfer from the main circulating collection. Canisius College does not actively solicit donations for Special Collections, realizing that there are still costs associated with processing and displaying material even if the material arrives free. Gifts are acceptable if they complement the collection. The Library does not conduct financial appraisals of material offered for donation. A decision to transfer a book from the main circulating collection into Special Collections is made o n the basis of either the book's inherent local value, its content, or its physical condition (ie. Fragility). Inclusion of materials in Special Collections is determined on a case-by-case basis and is at the sole discretion of the Library.

Accessibility

Special Collections is available for viewing or visiting by anyone expressing an interest in doing so. Appointments are encouraged. All items housed in Special Collections are cataloged in CanDO, the Canisius College Library's online catalog. They are also cataloged in OCLC's WorldCat, a worldwide online database of over thirty million bibliographic items. In addition, several notable ite ms, prinicipally the Books of Hours, are listed in both the 1940 print Census of Medieval and Renaissance Manuscripts in the United States and Canada (New York: H. W. Wilson) and in the Union Manuscript Computer Catalogue (http://members.aol.com/dericci/u mcc/umcc.html). Web pages describing the collection and offering sample graphical representations of works in the collection can be found on the Canisius College Library web page at http://www.canisius.edu/canhp/canlib/speccoll.htm

Karen Bordonaro

November 1999

COLLECTION DEVELOPMENT POLICY
Moravian College

Introduction

Reeves Library's collection and services are central to the educational mission of Moravian College and Moravian Theological Seminary. This collection development policy will address the needs of Moravian College. The collection development policy for Moravian Theological Seminary is appended. (Appendix 1)

Reeves Library's collection has always reflected the curriculum. Areas of strength have traditionally been American and British literature, American history, psychology, and art. Other areas of the collection have grown and/or and been weeded as the curriculum has changed. As Reeves Library is not a research library, no attempt is made to build a comprehensive collection. Current new areas of interest are nursing, China, and Latin American history.

The materials budget is divided by departments. Within departments individual faculty members are responsible for ordering for their students' needs. The librarians are responsible for the reference collection and for overall collection balance. Ultimate responsibility lies with the Library Director. The library welcomes purchase suggestions from administrators, students, staff, alumni, and other users.

Freedom of expression and free dissemination of all ideas are guiding principles of Reeves Library collection development. Intellectual freedom and opposition to censorship are essential components. The American Library Association's "Library Bill of Rights" is appended. (Appendix 2) In addition, Reeves Library fully supports copyright principles. (Appendix 3)

Resource sharing has an impact on collection development decisions. Reeves Library has cooperative borrowing agreements with Lehigh Valley Association of Independent Colleges and Southeast Pennsylvania Theological Library Association libraries, and Moravian students can borrow from the Bethlehem Area Public Library. In addition, the inter-library loan service makes millions of items available at little or no cost. We must keep accreditation factors in mind when deciding what materials to purchase and what we can borrow from other libraries.

Goals

The overall goal is a relevant collection of high quality.

A primary goal is to support the class work and research needs of the students. Students include undergraduates, MBA and Education Masters graduate students, and continuing education students. The undergraduates tend to be traditional college-age young adults; the graduate students and continuing education students tend to be older adults. Materials purchased should be at college level and above.

1

Another important goal is to support faculty needs. These include classroom-related research, class preparation materials, and current awareness. Reeves Library's collection is not intended to support faculty research. The library offers unlimited interlibrary loan support for faculty research needs.

Low priority goals include providing recreational materials and popular reading. The best-seller collection, popular books on tape, travel guides, healthy living and other how-to books are examples.

Material types
Traditionally the collection has been paper-based with a relatively small number of microforms, audio-and videocassettes, and computer discs.

Electronic formats
More recently, electronic formats have taken an important place in collection development. Remote databases have become the standard for student research. Full text articles and ejournals are often available. In some fields, e.g. computer science, the need for paper-based material is disappearing.

Reeves Library is attempting to keep up with this trend. Because electronic materials tend to cost more, this trend has had a big impact on our materials budget. Paper-based budgets have been static for several years while the electronic resources budget continues to grow.

Electronic resources are purchased with basic collection development principles in mind.

Videocassettes and DVDs
Reeves Library has recently taken on the management of the Media Center collection and budget. This collection is mostly videocassettes with a small number of DVDs. In the future, we will be concentrating on purchasing material on DVDs instead of videocassettes because the technology is changing. Standard collection development principles apply.

Serials
Under current budget restraints Reeves Library can add a new periodical only if an old one of comparable value is dropped. Titles must be indexed; otherwise they are of no value to students. Ejournals will continue to increase in number and importance in the collection.

The Serials Librarian will work with the faculty to constantly evaluate the collection for relevance to the curriculum and make changes where needed. Titles should be peer-reviewed and cost must be taken into consideration.

2

Moravian College

Keeping accreditation factors in mind, decisions on purchasing and retention of periodicals can be made relative to the availability of titles at local colleges.

Single issues or volumes and short, incomplete runs will not be added or retained.

Other formats
Information in any format will be added to the collection provided it meets our collection development standards. These formats include microfilm and microfiche, audiocassettes, maps, scores, CDs, computer files, etc.

In general, Reeves Library does not collect pamphlets, objects, or other ephemera.

Selection criteria to be considered
- Pertinence to the curriculum
- Reviewed by peers in the field
- Accurate and authoritative content
- At college reading level
- Represents alternative viewpoints
- Scarcity of material in a subject area
- Cost

Specific areas
- Languages. Reeves Library collects materials primarily in English. In addition, the library collects material in all languages with emphasis on those foreign languages taught here.
- In general, duplicate copies will not be added. The library will not purchase duplicates of classroom material that should be purchased by students.
- In general, textbooks will not be purchased.
- Trade paperbacks are usually preferred over hardbacks unless heavy use is anticipated. Popular paperbacks, including children's titles, are not purchased because they do not withstand wear. Exceptions are made as needed.
- Out-of-print materials will be added as needed. The Internet has made locating out-of-print titles easy to do.
- Superseded editions will not be retained.
- Material will be purchased to be put on Reserve as needed.
- The library does not collect local, state or federal documents.
- The gift policy is appended. (Appendix 4)
- A small collection of children's literature is maintained in support of the elementary education curriculum. Emphasis is on Newbery, Caldecott, and other award winners.
- A small collection of educational curriculum materials is maintained in support of the education curriculum.
- At this time ebooks (CD or other format) are not being added to the collection because the technology is still changing and is not currently suited to library use.

3

Collection Development Policies 119

They will be reconsidered in the future. Online subscription access to ebooks is also a possibility for the future.

Collection maintenance

Reeves Library staff will mend items that are in need of simple repairs. We will rebind books as needed. Items in need of extensive repair will be discarded and replaced. If an item is too important to discard and cannot be replaced, it will be housed in the Rare Books Room.

The weeding policy is appended. (Appendix 5)

This collection development policy should be revisited and revised on a regular and timely basis.

Appendixes:
1. Moravian Theological Seminary Collection Development Policy
2. Library Bill of Rights
3. Copyright Guidelines
4. Gift Policy
5. Weeding Policy
6. Library Mission Statement
7. Archives Statement

RB
8/15/02
10/18/02 rev.

4

Collection Development Policy

I. Mission

The mission of the North Central College Archives is to collect, organize, describe, preserve and make available for research materials on the history of the College and the local area as related to the College. The Archives supports the College community's need for historical information and provides reference assistance to archival researchers on and off campus. The Archives does not function as the repository for current College records.

II. Selection Responsibility

Selection is the responsibility of the Archivist/Associate Director of Archives. Approval of selections is the responsibility of the Director of Library Services.

III. Selection Criteria

Materials donated for inclusion in the College Archives must meet the following criteria:

1. **Scope**

    - Materials related to Plainfield College, North-Western College, and North Central College and its relationships with the external community.

    - Only non-active College records of permanent historic value.

2. **Subject Areas**

    - College community, including administration, faculty, staff, students, alumni, and trustees. (Archives selectively collects personal papers)

    - College business, including operation and administration, curriculum, programs, and activities.

    - College curriculum.

    - College programs and activities.

3. **Condition**

- The Archives will only accept items in good condition. Any exception requires the availability of conservation funds prior to acquisition.

4. **Format**

- Materials are collected by the Archives based on informational content rather than format.

- Formats may include, but are not limited to papers, photographs, publications, videotapes and films, sound recordings, digital or electronic, and artifacts.

- Due to space considerations, artifacts will undergo the strictest scrutiny before acceptance.

- The Archives does not accept unidentified photographs, unidentified or loose news clippings, or textbooks.

5. **Languages**

Relevant materials in any language are collected.

6. **Quantity**

The Archives collects original materials. In the case of printed materials and photographs that are not easily reproducible, the Archives collects two copies. Exceptions may be made at the discretion of the Archivist.

IV. **Acquisition**

A. **Gifts**

The Archives only accepts gifts that meet the selection criteria outlined in this policy and for which the donor has completed a "Deed of Gift". The "Deed of Gift" designates legal transfer of ownership, researcher access and copyright restrictions.

B. **Purchases**

The Archives does not usually purchase materials.

C.   **Transfers**

The Archives accepts transfers from College offices as outlined in the *Records Retention Schedule* for that office. The Archives will only accept non-current College records that have been deemed of permanent historic value to the College. The Archives will not accept materials that have been scheduled for disposal.

V.   **Deselection**

The Archives may deselect any materials that do not meet the selection criteria outlined in this policy.

VI.   **Policy Revisions**

This policy will be reviewed at least every five years by the Archivist and Director of Library Services.

kjb/cas
11/02

University of Saint Thomas

Department of Special Collections
University of St. Thomas Libraries
Collection Development Statement (rev. 6/2002)

I. Purpose of Collection

The mission of the Department of Special Collections is to identify, select, preserve, create access to, provide reference assistance to and promote the use of the rare and unique materials of the UST Libraries as well as the historical records of the University of St. Thomas. These collections support the research interests of university administrative departments and several university academic departments (Catholic Studies, English, Irish Studies, History) as well as researchers from around the world.

II. Areas for Collection

Celtic Collection

Founded on three significant donations from the Ancient Order of Hibernians (1917), the Peter O'Connor Family (1936) and the Foxley family gift of the Eamon O'Toole Library (1956), the Celtic collection documents the history, culture, and literature of the Celtic peoples (Irish, Scot, Welch, Manx, and Breton). The collection is especially strong in its holdings of Irish local history and politics, folklore, modern Irish poetry and Irish/Scots Gaelic language.

With the assistance, of the Kennedy and Ryan endowed funds, the department continues to purchase books to enhance the strengths of this collection. Where appropriate, the Department seeks manuscript collections that complement the strengths of the book collections.

Bach-Dunn Luxembourgiana Collection

Founded in 1993 through a gift from the Luxembourg Heritage Society, the collection seeks to document the history, culture and language of the people of the Grand-Duchy of Luxembourg and Americans of Luxembourg heritage living in the United States.

With the assistance of the Luxembourg endowed fund, the department continues to purchase books to enhance the strengths of this collection. Additionally, the Department will seek manuscript collections that complement the strengths of the book collection.

Chesterton-Belloc Collection

Founded on two significant donations of the works of Hilaire Belloc (1984) and G. K. Chesterton (1991), the Chesterton-Belloc collection composes a nearly complete set of first editions by these English-Catholic writers.

With the assistance of the Kellen endowed fund, the department continues to purchase newly published and older editions by Chesterton and Belloc in an attempt to develop a comprehensive collection of their published works.

Christopher Dawson Collection

In 1996, the Center for Catholic Studies at the University of St. Thomas purchased the papers and scholarly library of the English Catholic historian Christopher Dawson. The papers and the library were deposited with the Department of Special Collections where the books were cataloged and the papers were arranged for scholarly research.

While the department is committed to maintaining this collection, there is no attempt made to enhance this collection.

Franz Mueller Library

In 1998, the personal library of Franz Mueller, retired University of St. Thomas economics professor was acquired by the Department of Special Collections. The collection is especially strong in German-language materials related Mueller's study of the work of Heinrich Pesch and other areas of economic thought.

While the department is committed to maintaining this collection, there is no attempt made to enhance its holdings.

French Memoir Collection

The French Memoir Collection consists of a group of approximately 300 French-language volumes which came to the University in 1918-1919 from the estates of Archbishop John Ireland and Fr. William Etzel (the college's first librarian). The works are mainly 18th and 19th century editions of journals, letters and memoirs from the French Court and aristocracy covering the period 1500 - 1815.

While the department is committed to maintaining this collection, no attempt will be made to enhance its holdings.

University Archives

The University Archives serves as the official repository for the permanent records of the University of St. Thomas and its environs (including the St. Paul Seminary, the St. John Vianney Seminary, the Catholic Digest [through 2001], and the St. Thomas Military Academy [through 1965] and the Nazareth Hall Pro-Seminary [1923 - 1970]). It accessions, organizes, preserves and provides controlled access to those records which possess continuing historical, administrative, legal and fiscal value. These records are collected regardless of format (paper, electronic, audio-visual, microformat). Additionally, the University Archives will seek the scholarly papers of faculty members and alumni who are prominent in their fields.

University of Saint Thomas

The University Archive collects all theses, dissertations and master's level capstone papers produced by any graduate degree program of the University. The University Archives also seeks to purchase for its collection any book length monograph written by members of the faculty or staff of the University as well as any work relating to the history of the University.

III. Acquisition of New Materials

The Department of Special Collections will consider the acquisition of new collections under the following conditions:

1. The collection under consideration must reflect the existing subject strengths of the Department of Special Collections.

2. The collection must be substantial enough to provide a basis for scholarly research in a subject area.

3. Adequate funds must be available to insure that the collection can be maintained and developed.

4. There should be some relationship between the subject matter of the collection and the curriculum of the university.

5. Realia and artifacts are not collected.

6. Works of art being offered for acquisition will be referred to the Executive Vice President's Office.

Comments, questions, or feedback can be directed to libweb@stthomas.edu
© 1996-2004 University of St. Thomas Libraries.
St. Paul - Minneapolis, MN. All rights reserved.
http://www.stthomas.edu/libraries

The University of Tennessee at Martin
Paul Meek Library
Museum, Special Collections, University Archives
Scope Statement and Collection Policies

The Jimmie and Alliene Corbitt Special Collections and Archives (the Collection) is a departmental unit of the Paul Meek Library on the campus of the University of Tennessee at Martin. As a unit, Special Collections' mission is to identify, acquire, preserve, and make available to its readership documentary materials of archival value relative to the University of Tennessee at Martin and its predecessor, and similar historical and cultural materials that fall under the venues of its three respective sections, focusing on northwest Tennessee and the river counties of western Kentucky.

The department is divided into three sections, each with an independent but collectively related scope, described in detail below: Special Collections, University Archives, and University Museum.

General Collection Guidelines

All material housed in units of the Collection are governed by the following guidelines:

a. *Language*   English is the predominant language of the region and institution, therefore materials will be secured primarily in English. Germane works in other languages may be acquired, and an effort will be made to acquire a contemporary copy in English as well.

b. *Format*   To facilitate preservation, photographs, manuscripts, books, and realia will be housed separately. Materials in all documentary formats may be acquired, with preference being given to the format of first publication or initial release. For various mechanically mediated formats (magnetic and digital recordings, microcard, microfiche, etc.) the long-term cost and viability of maintaining necessary hardware for archival stability, playback, and duplication *must* be considered on an equal footing with the content of the record. Reformatting to an eye-readable format from electronic/microreproduction originals is acceptable and may be necessary. Specific exceptions to this apply: newspapers will—with isolated exceptions—be retained and provided to researchers only on microfilm; census records will be provided on microfilm.

c. *Donations*   Under the terms outlined herein for its sections, Special Collections will accept materials from alumni, faculty, other institutions, and from the public at large. Each bequest, gift, donation, or purchase must meet the standards enumerated for the section to which it will belong. No materials will be transferred, housed, accepted, or acquired without the prior approval of the Special Collections librarian/archivist. All donations should be accompanied by completed acquisition documentation, including requisite deed and release forms, at the time of donation. *No manuscript material under any circumstance will be accepted without a deed of gift properly signed by the donor and/or the legal owner, or a dated letter of intention specifically covering the intended gift materials.* As stipulated in the deed documentation, title to any donated material is transferred irrevocably to the institution. The Curator reserves the right to reject any material in an acquisition if it falls beyond scope. Decisions affecting housing and storage, arrangement and description, display, publication, and outreach for donated materials rest solely with the Curator on behalf of the institution. Gifts of books will be accepted only without strictures on their disposition; manuscripts with a term of closure imposed by the donor will not be accepted if the closure terms are longer than 25 years unless the curator judges the content to have overwhelming historical significance.

d. *Retention*   Material with topics judged by the Curator to be beyond the scope of the Collection may be separated and disposed of (transferred, discarded) during processing. Out-of-scope material will be retained only with a view towards its value in dispersal. Materials already existing in the Collection may be re-evaluated and be removed from holdings (if monographic) or have parts thereof removed (if a manuscript collection) if a donor agreement does not specifically prohibit such dismissals.

e. *Location*   Materials from the various units will be housed in storage facilities under the control of the Paul Meek Library or by the University of Tennessee at Martin and serviced by the Corbitt Special Collections staff.

f. *Circulation*   All departmental materials are non-circulating but may be used by patrons in the service points during open hours and may be exhibited. Duplicate copies may be found in more than one area of the department, or in the Library's circulating collection. Bound volumes generally are not available on Interlibrary Loan services, but may be loaned to qualified institutions for exhibitions. All loans must be documented. Microfilm and manuscript material may not be loaned.

g. *Duplication*   A microfilm reader/printer is available in the NTHSC; photocopying from bound volumes, manuscripts, and University Archives is done for patrons on request, provided the limits of U.S. Code Title 17 (copyright) are not infringed. The Curator may deny duplication requests to preserve the material, or because of donor restrictions, or due to Library or university policy.

<u>Scope Statements for Individual Sections</u>

<u>Special Collections</u>
Special Collections comprise the department's holdings of non-archival photographic, manuscript, monographic, and serial materials. It is divided into several units that serve different topical and administrative functions.

Northwest Tennessee Heritage Study Center collection   This unit includes primary service copies works (primarily monographs but also serials) relating to the natural and social history and governance of our core region, defined by the state as Northwest Tennessee (Dyer, Crockett, Gibson, Henry, Carroll, Benton, Lake, Obion, and Weakley counties) and Kentucky's Hickman, Carlisle, and Fulton counties. We will collect all records in any format relating to this core area. Beyond this, the collection will include materials documenting the local and general history of west Tennessee; and the natural, local, and social history and genealogy of the state of Tennessee. Special emphasis is placed on acquiring local histories and genealogical sources, and the military history of units and combatants from Tennessee or which fought here during the U.S. Civil War. Works relating to the state that do not fall under these categories (such as fiction) will be housed in the department's General Stacks. State and local history materials acquired by the Department and housed elsewhere in the library because of record type (such as microfilmed newspapers, city directories, or county censuses) fall within this collection policy.

For areas beyond Tennessee's boundaries, emphasis is placed on acquiring printed materials of genealogical importance to the core region (as defined above). Monographic works and periodicals from any time period may be acquired if deemed significant to the collection and worth preservation. The main emphasis will be on acquiring in-print publications and reprints of earlier genealogical reference works. Resources will be expended only for works of a general nature in the field of genealogy and on items within the regional focus; works from any time or relative to any location may be included in the collection as gifts. Microfilmed primary sources, such as state and federal census records, will be included in the collection as available.

With the exception of periodicals, genealogical materials relating to Tennessee will be housed in the regional heritage collection.

Both current and out-of-print titles are acquired, including original impressions and reprinted editions when possible. Reproductions, including photocopy, are secured when the originals are unavailable and when copyright laws are not infringed. If the Library holds both a reproduction copy and an original volume, the original will be removed to either the Special Collections general stacks or Rare Books at the curator's discretion. Relevant materials with substantial intrinsic value are housed in the Rare Books unit and will be subject to the strictures covering the use of those materials.

General Stacks ("Special Collections")   Books received by gift or purchase that fall within the scope of the department but do not fit within the scope of a specific collection are housed in the General Stacks. Works relating specifically to the state's antiquities will be housed here, as will Tennessee as a subject of fiction and popular nonfiction, but these holdings will be limited to works actually dealing with regions within the state of Tennessee or the state as a whole. Older books judged worth keeping but which might be at risk for damage or theft in the Library's circulating collection may be housed in Special Collections' General Stacks.

Rare Books   Holdings are limited to monographs acquired by purchase or gift which have a substantial intrinsic value or for which very few copies (fewer than six) are recorded as held in other U.S. or Canadian institutions. The exception to this is the Harry Harrison Kroll materials, which are housed in rare books because of the nature of the materials as a group. The Collection does not seek to acquire rare books beyond the scope of the collection's general guidelines, but will accept them as gifts.

University Archives

The holdings of University Archives are limited to "records" (documentary materials generated in the conduct of business) of departments and offices of the institution now known as the University of Tennessee at Martin, together with that of its predecessor, the Hall-Moody Institute. Such records may be published or unpublished, and may be in any recording format, including photographs. As a state institution, the laws of Tennessee that govern retention and access to public records are in force, including the federal Freedom of Information Act. Specifically excluded from archival holdings are the records and data maintained by the University Registrar's office.

Unless they consist primarily of institutional administrative materials, faculty papers deemed worth retention will be housed in the manuscripts section. Campus organizations not funded by the university or state will be accepted and housed as manuscript collections.

University Museum

The Museum serves primarily as an exhibit venue and maintains no collection of its own. The Museum does not actively acquire material by purchase or gift.

COLLECTION POLICY

ARCHIVES AND SPECIAL COLLECTIONS

A. Archives

The Archivist of the College actively collects and preserves the archives of Wabash College in the Ramsay Archival Center. These records may include papers, books, audio and video cassettes, film, photographs, recordings, microfilm, artifacts, and other formats that document the life of the college, both past and present. The Archivist consults with individuals and departments concerning retention of College records as the need arises.

B. Special Collections

Materials are evaluated and placed in the protective environment of Special Collections for the following reasons:
    a. Subject matter relates to the history of the college and/or the curriculum
    b. Unique and/or rare titles
    c. Special bindings
    d. First editions by faculty, staff, or alumni authors
    e. Early imprints.

The College does not actively seek acquisition of special collections from donors outside the college, but may accept such gifts if the collection fits within our collecting scope. Purchases for Special Collections are made at the recommendation of the Archivist, Librarians, and/or faculty, with funding handled through the general library acquisitions budget.

Williams College Archives and Special Collections

Collection Development Policy

Introduction

The collection development policy of Williams College Archives and Special Collections is planned to serve as a tool to guide the department's staff in making informed decisions regarding potential acquisitions. The policy is, therefore, a component of the department's appraisal process through which material is acquired for the College's collections. The guidelines also seek to ensure an appropriate balance between the department's resources and its commitments.

Statement of Purpose

Williams College Archives and Special Collections was established to appraise, collect, organize, describe, preserve, and make available the College's records of permanent administrative, legal, fiscal and historical value. The Archives also serves as a repository for non-official historical materials relating to the history of the College, its founders, faculty, students, administrators, staff and alumni. In addition, the department administers several of the College's special collections, most notably the Paul Whiteman Collection, the Shaker Collection, and Sawyer Library's rare book collections.

As part of its mission, the Archives provides facilities for the retention, preservation, and research use of its collections. The department serves as a research center for the study of the College's history, and for the investigation of select topics of regional, national or international significance. Collections are made available, College and donor restrictions permitting, to members of the College community, as well as undergraduate and graduate students, scholars, and serious researchers from the general public.

The Archives serves in a public relations capacity by promoting knowledge and understanding of the origins, programs and goals of the College, and strengthens the College's involvement in the study of primary historical sources. The department accomplishes these goals through the acquisition, processing and preservation of collections; its reference and research services; and such outreach activities as the development and installation of exhibitions, the production of publications in a variety of formats, and offering tours, classes and workshops dealing with topics such as the history of the College, research methods, preservation management and conservation techniques, and archival programming.

General Collecting Guidelines

In general, the department collects in areas that:
- support the Archives' existing collections;
- extend the Archives' research strengths, interests, and needs;
- support the College's curriculum and the research interests of its students and faculty;
- anticipate future research needs;
- show a high ratio of use to volume, condition, and processing costs; and

- complement rather than compete with the collecting priorities of other regional special collections repositories

Acquisitions are normally made through transfer from a College office or department, donation, or purchase. If the donation is of original unpublished material, a legal deed of gift or release is sought from the donor. Prospective donors of material outside the scope of the Collection Policy will normally be referred to other repositories that collect in the area/s described by that material.

College Archives: the official records

As part of its mission, the Archives collects and preserves College records possessing permanent administrative, legal, fiscal and historical value. The purpose of collecting such records is to provide documentation of the development and growth of the College, in particular its primary functions of teaching and research, its role in the community at large, the activities of its student body and alumni, and the development of its physical plant and grounds. Records are also collected in order to adhere to federally- and state-mandated records retention requirements.

The Archives works with offices and departments of the College to appraise the records that they create in the course of their activities and to select those that should be preserved for future use. Priority is given to those records that reflect the activities of College officers and committees that formulate or approve College or division-wide policy as well as faculty and administrative involvement in these activities.

Recorded information documenting College activities is collected regardless of format, and may include: administrative papers and files; publications, reports, and other printed material; financial and legal materials; microforms; computer tape, files and discs; photographs, slides and other pictorial material; maps and blueprints; sound recordings; motion picture film and video tape; and ephemera and memorabilia.

Archival records deemed not of permanent value are held in storage until they can be legally destroyed by shredding or incineration, depending upon the information contained in those records.

Williamsiana: supporting historical materials

The department acquires a wide variety of historical material, or "Williamsiana," to support and augment the official records of the College. This material may include, but is not limited to: manuscripts, student theses, visual materials, oral histories, artifacts, works published by faculty and alumni, student newspapers and periodicals, local history collections, and published reference works.

Manuscripts – The department collects manuscript material, including:
- students' personal papers, especially those that illuminate life at the College;
- personal and professional papers of Williams faculty and administrators that document their teaching, administrative and/or research careers and the development of the College's curriculum;
- records of clubs, societies and institutes established and maintained by Williams students and other College personnel;

- papers of select noted alumni, especially those who have been active in the areas of missionary work and the ministry, international affairs, and higher education;
- course syllabi
- materials relating to the Williams family, the French and Indian War in our extended geographic area, and the founding of the College;
- Bachelor's theses in all disciplines and the major papers of students in the Development Economics course (Master's theses in Art History are maintained by the Clark Art Institute Library, and papers in other undergraduate courses are ordinarily not acquired unless they document a significant shift in curricular trends).

Visual Material – The department acquires a variety of visual material, including photographs in all formats, slides, negatives, films, videos, prints, scrapbooks, albums, postcards, and letterheads. Subject matter must relate to Williams College, our geographic area, or the lives of our students, staff and faculty. Every effort is made to forward offers of fine art, such as oil portraits and exclusive printings of intaglio or lithographic processes, to the Williams College Museum of Art.

Oral Histories – The Archives maintains the tapes, transcripts, and records produced by the College's Oral History Program, and may accept oral histories of Williams individuals produced by other Williams College students, faculty or staff, or by other colleges and universities.

Artifacts – Artifacts are acquired for the College's historical collections if the Archives judges it can properly preserve and provide access to them. Items must document College life or the careers of our alumni. Due to storage and preservation issues, offers of fine and decorative arts are normally forwarded to the Williams College Museum of Art.

Published Works – Acquired and/or made available are published works, regardless of format, which concern the history of the College, its alumni, faculty and staff, and our geographic area. These may include:
- newspapers, journals, magazines, handbooks and yearbooks produced by the student body, student clubs, and alumni classes;
- material pertaining to the history of our local geographic area, especially that which supports inquiries into the relations between the College and its community (in this area, every effort is made to complement rather than complete with the Williamstown House of Local History);
- works authored by tenured members of the faculty;
- works by Williams alumni, especially if they relate to missionary work or the ministry, international affairs, higher education or the history of Williams College;
- biographies and autobiographies of Williams alumni, staff, faculty and donors;
- reference works and databases that support research performed with primary sources.

Special Collections

The Special Collections arm of the department supports several topical collections with few or no connections to the history of Williams College.

Rare book collections – Special Collections maintains materials acquired by the College Library that are deemed rare and/or difficult to replace due to their value, age, condition, format or subject matter. In addition, the department collects books and pamphlets, from primarily the 18th-through the present, in such topical areas as:
- international law and diplomacy,

- William Cullen Bryant,
- Assamese language, literature and culture,
- the French and Indian War,
- life, especially missionary activities and education, in 19th-century Hawaii, and
- slavery and abolition in the United States.

Special Collections also maintains the libraries of the Philologian and Philotechnican Societies, comprising titles acquired by the student members of this literary and debating club.

Paul Whiteman Collection -- The department collects material that directly documents the life and career of Paul Whiteman, and may acquire collections pertaining to the careers of associated composers, arrangers and band members as they relate to Whiteman. Such material may include manuscripts, pictorial material, motion picture film and videos, sound recordings, ephemera and research materials.

Shaker Collection -- Special Collections acquires material produced from the 18th- through the 20th-centuries both by and about the Shakers. Acquisitions may include manuscripts, photographs, microforms, printed material and ephemera, and are especially sought in the areas of:

- general Shaker theology,
- the history of the New Lebanon community,
- spirit messages, and
- Shaker hymnals.

Cooperative Agreements

While the Archives maintains no official cooperative acquisitions agreements, the department works unofficially with other repositories and College offices to ensure that prospective donations are offered to the institution/office that may best be able to preserve the material and to provide access to it. Institutions and offices with which the Archives currently works closely include the Chapin Library of Rare Books and Manuscripts, the Williams College Museum of Art, and the Williamstown House of Local History.

Policy Review and De-accession

The Collection Development Policy will be reviewed periodically to ensure that it reflects the College's collecting needs. If at any time donated material is deemed outside the scope of the Archives' collecting plan or otherwise unsuitable for the collections, it will be considered for de-accession. The Archives will normally consider several options for de-accession: return of the material to the donor, return of the material to the donor's family, donation of the material to another repository, or destruction of the material.

Reviewed by Phyllis Cutler, College Librarian
5/27/98

GIFT POLICIES

Archives and Special Collections Gift Policy

Over the years, the Archives & Special Collections at Franklin & Marshall College has grown from the generous donation of material and financial gifts. Alumni, faculty, private organizations, and members of the public have all given generously in support of the college's mission. The Shadek-Fackenthal Library continues to welcome such gifts, and hopes you will consider contributing to the educational and historical value of the collections.

- **What the Library Collects**
- **What the Library Does Not Collect**
- **Access to Materials**
- **Care of Materials**
- **Copyright and Tax Considerations**
- **Making a Gift**
- **Deed of Gift**

What the Library Collects

Archives & Special Collections seeks materials that match aspects of the following subject areas:

African American History
Art of the Book
Autographs
Classical Literature
Exploration - 19th Century
Franklin & Marshall Academy History
Franklin & Marshall College History
German American Imprints
History of Science
Incunabula
Items relating to Benjamin Franklin
Items relating to John Marshall
Jewish American History
Lexicography
Lincolniana
Literary Papers
Local History, Lancaster City, PA
Local History, Lancaster County, PA
Military History
Napoleonana
Pennsylvania Civil War History
Pennsylvania German Culture
Theater, Television, and Film
Women's History

Archives & Special Collections collects materials of the following types/formats:

Autographs
Broadsides
Carte-des-Visites
Correspondence (personal and professional)
Diaries/ Journals
Drafts of creative works
Films/ Videotapes
Financial Records
Fraktur
Legal Records
Maps
Memoirs/ Reminiscences
Microfilm/Microform
Newsletters
Organizational Publications
Office Files
Oral History Tapes/ Transcripts
Pamphlets/ Brochures
Photographs
Postcards
Posters
Prints
Rare Books
Reports
Scrapbooks
Sheet Music
Sound Recordings
Speeches/ Lectures

Please Note: New collections that may support the mission of the college will also be considered with great interest. For a complete understanding of current collecting priorities, please consult the **Collection Development Policy** of Archives and Special Collections.

What the Library Does Not Collect

Archives and Special Collections does not collect any and all items relating to American History, common reproductions of historical documents, decorative arts artifacts, and local genealogical materials.

Access to Materials

The Shadek-Fackenthal Library abides by the American Library Association/Society of American Archivists' 1994 **Joint Statement on Access to Original Research Materials**.

The Archives & Special Collections of Franklin & Marshall College can only accept items when they are donated free and clear of all restrictions. Materials will not be accepted with restrictions as to use, secure storage, or future disposition.

Care of Materials

When the Archives & Special Collections adds gift materials to its holdings, it takes care to ensure their long-term preservation and to make them accessible to students, faculty, and professional researchers. All materials are housed in secure areas under environmentally controlled conditions. Items do not circulate outside the Archives and Special Collections Reading Area. Acid-free boxes, folders, and other containers are employed to house materials, and item-level conservation steps are taken when appropriate. To enhance the research use of materials, collections are arranged, described, and cataloged in accordance with nationally recognized library and archival standards. To promote widespread awareness of holdings, the Shadek-Fackenthal Library makes descriptions of collections available on its website, in the Franklin & Marshall online catalog, and through national directories such as **Archives USA**.

Copyright and Tax Considerations

Copyright

Preferably, copyright remains with the donor and/or donor's heirs, subject to copyright ownership and renewals. The statement on copyright within the **Deed of Gift** should be addressed at the time of transfer. For additional information regarding copyright and public domain, please see the following websites:

- **Copyright Office**, located within the Library of Congress
- **When Works Pass Into the Public Domain**, provided by the University of North Carolina

Tax Considerations

In compliance with the current tax law, the Library does not provide appraisals for gifts received. The appraisal of a gift to the Library for tax purposes is the responsibility of the donor who benefits from the tax deduction.

Making a Gift

If you are interested in making a material or financial gift to the Archives & Special Collections, please stop by the Shadek-Fackenthal Library, or contact librarian Christopher Raab with a description of the potential gift.

Christopher Raab
Archives & Special Collections Librarian
Shadek-Fackenthal Library
Franklin & Marshall College
P.O. Box 3003
Lancaster, PA 17604-3003

Please Note: For UPS/FedEx packages, please substitute the following street address for P.O. Box 3003:

450 College Avenue

Telephone (717) 291-4225

Email **christopher.raab@fandm.edu**

Deed of Gift

A **Deed of Gift** will be discussed with the donor, and signed by all parties upon transfer of the materials. The Deed of Gift addresses the following legal concerns:

1. Statement as to the ownership of the physical materials.
2. Statement as to the administration and use of the materials.
3. Statement as to the ownership of literary rights.
4. Statement as to the disposition of materials not retained upon final review.

A sample copy of our **Deed of Gift** form can be provided upon request.

Thank you for considering the Archives & Special Collections at Franklin & Marshall College.

Return to Policies and Services

Return to top of page

12/17/02 - cmr
rev. 03/17/03

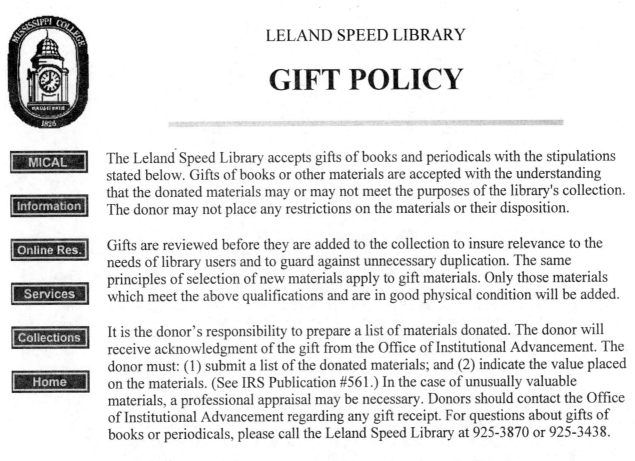

LELAND SPEED LIBRARY

GIFT POLICY

The Leland Speed Library accepts gifts of books and periodicals with the stipulations stated below. Gifts of books or other materials are accepted with the understanding that the donated materials may or may not meet the purposes of the library's collection. The donor may not place any restrictions on the materials or their disposition.

Gifts are reviewed before they are added to the collection to insure relevance to the needs of library users and to guard against unnecessary duplication. The same principles of selection of new materials apply to gift materials. Only those materials which meet the above qualifications and are in good physical condition will be added.

It is the donor's responsibility to prepare a list of materials donated. The donor will receive acknowledgment of the gift from the Office of Institutional Advancement. The donor must: (1) submit a list of the donated materials; and (2) indicate the value placed on the materials. (See IRS Publication #561.) In the case of unusually valuable materials, a professional appraisal may be necessary. Donors should contact the Office of Institutional Advancement regarding any gift receipt. For questions about gifts of books or periodicals, please call the Leland Speed Library at 925-3870 or 925-3438.

Source: Board of Trustees, Dec. 10, 1998

Library Information Menu   Acquisitions & Collection Development

Return to Speed Library Home Page
Last updated: September 4, 2001

Archives and Special Collections

Home | General Services | Reference | Browse Collection | Donating Collections | Exhibits and Projects

Donations > Donating Rare Books

Why Donate?

The Archives and Special Collections collect rare books related to a wide variety of areas, fields and disciplines. The rare book collection serves as a primary resource for teaching and research conducted by student, faculty and other researchers. Donations to this collection, or monetary donations for the purchase of rare books, help us to increase the breadth and depth of our collections and thus allows us to better support the curricular needs of the College.

What Should I Donate?

The Archives and Special Collections main areas of collecting include: American history, illustrated editions of Dante Alighieri's *Divina commedia,* 19th century text books which are known to have been used in the courses of study at Mount Holyoke Female Seminary, rare children's books, published works related the Collège de 'pataphysique, Renaissance Science books, and fine press books. Because our collections cover more than these main areas, gifts of books that fall outside of these areas will be considered on an individual basis. Both small, single volume, or larger, multi-volume, donations will be considered.

How Do I Make A Donation?

The first step in making a donation is to contact the Rare Books Librarian. In case of relatively local or large donations, the Archives Special Collections staff may wish to see them before they are physically transferred.

Monetary Appraisal for Tax Deductions

Donors may be able to take a tax deduction for the donation of rare books. Donors wishing to have more information on this matter should speak with either a tax consultant or an attorney. College policy prohibits the Archives and Special Collections from providing monetary valuations of collections. Donors wishing to hire an appraiser can contact the Archives and Special Collections for a list of for-hire appraisers.

Care for Collections

The Archives and Special Collections is managed by professional archivists and librarians whose first priority is preservation of and access to rare and historic materials. The Archives and Special Collection staff arrange, describe and catalog collections to ensure ease of access by researchers.

Should a collection require repair or other conservation work the Archives and Special Collections will consult with professional conservators. All materials are stored in secure, climate-controlled areas. No primary source materials circulate and only Archives and Special Collections staff may retrieve materials for researchers.

Monetary Donations

In addition to accepting donations of rare books the Archives and Special Collections will also accept monetary donations toward the purchase of books, or the preservation of existing collections. All monetary donations are tax deductible.

Further Information

For further information on donating rare books to the Mount Holyoke College Archives and Special Collections, please contact the Director at:

Phone:(413) 538-2441   **E-mail:**jgking@mtholyoke.edu

Address:
Jennifer King
Mount Holyoke College
Archives and Special Collections
8C Dwight Hall
50 College St.
South Hadley, MA 01075

Home | MyMHC | Web Email | Directories | SiteMap | Search | Help

Admission | Academics | Campus Life | Athletics
Library & Technology | About the College | Alumnae | News & Events | Offices & Services

Mount Holyoke College

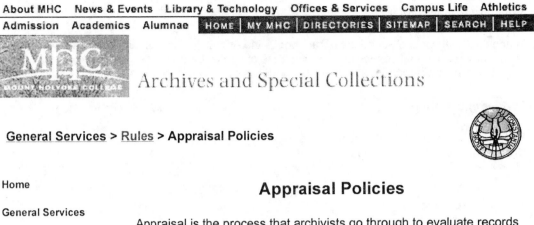

About MHC   News & Events   Library & Technology   Offices & Services   Campus Life   Athletics

Admission   Academics   Alumnae | HOME | MY MHC | DIRECTORIES | SITEMAP | SEARCH | HELP

Archives and Special Collections

General Services > Rules > Appraisal Policies

Home

General Services

Ready Reference

Browse Collections

Donating Papers & Books

Records Management

Exhibits and Projects

Search Services
[   ] GO

Additional Searches

Staff

Hours

Ask An Archivist

Site Directory

Five College Catalog

Five College Archives

Appraisal Policies

Appraisal is the process that archivists go through to evaluate records and documents for their continuing value. Appraisal is perhaps the most daunting and intellectually demanding task that archivists must undertake. Ultimately, the creation of a comprehensive historic record depends to a great extent on the care with which they have appraised the documents in their care. Because of this appraisal must be conducted in a consistent fashion and with a broad view. In an attempt to formalize the appraisal process at the Mount Holyoke College Archives and Special Collections we have laid out the following policies and procedures.

1. **Appraisal Criteria for College Records**
2. **Appraisal Criteria for Personal Papers**
3. **Document Type Lists**
4. **Deaccessioning Policy**

Home | MyMHC | Web Email | Directories | SiteMap | Search | Help

Admission | Academics | Campus Life | Athletics
Library & Technology | About the College | Alumnae | News & Events | Offices & Services

Copyright © 2004 Mount Holyoke College. This page created by Archives and Special Collections and maintained by Peter Carini. Last modified on July 16, 2004.

144 Gift Policies

Archives and Special Collections

Home | General Services | Reference | Browse Collection | Donating Collections | Exhibits and Projects

Donations > Personal Papers

Why Donate?

The Archives and Special Collections collect the papers and records of individuals, institutions and organizations associated with Mount Holyoke College. The records are maintained as primary resources for teaching and research. The manuscript collections document the social history of this country and other countries primarily as seen through the eyes of women and the educators of women. The collections also document the social history of Mount Holyoke College through the letters, diaries, photographs, scrapbooks and course records of faculty and students. Each year these collections are consulted by thousands of researchers from around the world. With the donation of each new collection, we are able to the increase the breadth and depth of our resources to better serve the educational needs of the College and of scholars who are drawn to our collections due to Mount Holyoke's prominent place in the history of women's education. Each donation helps to enlarge the documentation not only of the effect of Mount Holyoke on the world, but of the effect of individuals on the institution itself.

What Should I Donate?

While the Archives and Special Collections is always looking for large donations that document the life and work on an individual or the history of an institution/organization associated with the College, we are also happy to receive single items as well. In general the Archives and Special Collections staff prefer to work closely with donors to determine what records or documents within their papers have continuing historic interest prior to the donation of a collection. The importance of records and documents diminish if they are removed, reordered or rearranged. Donors are encouraged to contact the Archives and Special Collections prior to sorting or rearranging materials they wish to donate.

Below are two lists of some types of materials that are usually of historic value. Please note that this list is not definitive and there may be other types of documents or records not included here that may have continuing research value.

Personal and Family Papers:

Letters	Diaries	Scrapbooks
Speeches	Research Notes	Lecture Notes
Photo Albums	Photographs	Biographical Info.
Genealogical Info.	Professional Files	Video & Audio Tapes

Organization and Institutional Records:

Articles of Incorporation	By-laws	Annual Reports
Correspondence	Meeting Minutes	Legal Documents
Financial Documents	Planning Documents	Press Releases
Publications	Photographs	Video & Audio Tapes

How Do I Make A Donation?

Mount Holyoke College

The first step in making a donation is to contact the Director of Archives and Special Collections. In cases where the records are relatively local or are large in quantity, the Archives Special Collections staff may wish to see them before they are physically transferred. In such cases it is best that the records not be rearranged prior to inspection by the Archives and Special Collections. Arrangements can then be made for the physical transfer of the records.

Ownership of the records is transferred when the donor signs a deed of gift. While the deed of gift is a standard document, it can be customized to suite the needs of individual donors. In most cases the Archives and Special Collections will not accept gifts unless the ownership and copyright are transferred to Mount Holyoke College

Restrictions on Access

The Archives and Special Collections encourage full access to all manuscript collections. On occasion access to certain materials within a collection may be restricted for a set period of time. In these instances the Archives and Special Collections staff will discuss with the donor reasonable restrictions on access in accordance with the policies of the Archives and Special Collections.

Copyright

Copyright usually belongs to the creator of the records (letters, diaries, photographs, etc.). The Archives and Special Collections strongly encourage donors to consider transferring copyright of their papers to Mount Holyoke College. Transfer of copyright greatly assists researchers who might wish to quote or cite references in the collection.

Monetary Appraisal for Tax Deductions

Donors may be able to take a tax deduction for the donation of personal papers. Donors wishing to have more information on this matter should speak with either a tax consultant or an attorney. College policy prohibits the Archives and Special Collections from providing monetary valuations of collections. Donors wishing to hire an appraiser can contact the Archives and Special Collections for a list of for-hire manuscript appraisers.

Care for Collections

The Archives and Special Collections is managed by professional archivists and librarians whose first priority is preservation of and access to historic materials. The Archives and Special Collection staff arrange, describe and catalog collections to ensure ease of access by researchers.

Should a collection require repair or other conservation work the Archives and Special Collections will consult with professional conservators. All materials are stored in acid-free containers in secure, climate-controlled areas. No primary source materials circulate and only Archives and Special Collections staff may retrieve materials for researchers.

Monetary Donations

The cost of caring for, describing and giving access to rare and historic materials is extremely high. Donors are encouraged to consider making a monetary donation toward the arrangement, description and preservation of their donation.

Further Information

For further information on donating your papers or records to the Mount Holyoke College Archives and Special Collections, please contact the Director at:

Phone:(413) 538-2441   **E-mail:**jgking@mtholyoke.edu

Address:

146 Gift Policies

Jennifer King
Mount Holyoke College
Archives and Special Collections
8C Dwight Hall
50 College St.
South Hadley, MA 01075

Significant assistance with the text for this section came from *A Guide To Donating Your Personal or Family Papers to a Repository*, Society of American Archivists, 1994

Home | MyMHC | Web Email | Directories | SiteMap | Search | Help

Admission | Academics | Campus Life | Athletics
Library & Technology | About the College | Alumnae | News & Events | Offices & Services

DEED OF GIFT FORMS

Albion College

Please contact the Archivist first to make sure your gift fits into the collection development policy for either the College Archives, Rare Books collection, or West Michigan Conference United Methodist Church Archives before arranging to send your gift to Albion College. Once confirmation has been received, please print out this form, fill it out and send it in with your donation.

Special Collections Ho
[Click and Go!]

If you have a question
regarding
any of these materials,
please fill out the
Special Collections
Reference Request Foi

Deed of Gift

I, _____, hereby donate the materials described below to Albion College for inclusion in Albion College Special Collections. As sole owner of these materials, I donate physical ownership of them to Albion College, which shall occur upon delivery to the College. However, the donor, his/her heirs, and his/her estate shall retain title to such literary property rights (copyright) as he/she may possess unless otherwise stipulated below.

Description of Gift *(Office Use Only)*

Total Number of Boxes/Items _____

Inclusive Dates _____

Inventory Attached?   Yes   or   No

*Condition*_____

Subject
*Matter*_____

Arrangement

_____ Alphabetical   _____Numerical   _____ Chronological   _____
Topical

Physical Formats *Check all that apply*

_____ Correspondence   _____ Microfilm
_____ Photographs   _____ Institutional Records

Albion College

_____ Books		_____ Reports	
_____ Memorabilia		_____ Research Materials	
_____ Studies		_____ Publications	
_____ Conference Materials		_____ Slides	
_____ Film		_____ Sound Recordings	
_____ Video Recordings			

Copyright

I do not control copyright for any of the donated materials. To the best of my knowledge, the copyright is controlled by:

Name   _____

Address   _____

Phone Number   _____

If you wish to transfer, convey, and assign to Albion College, on behalf of Special Collections, any copyright which you control in the above-named materials, subject to the limitations, if any, stated below, please initial here _____

If you do not wish to transfer copyright, but give permission for the library to make copies for users of the materials, please initial here _____

Limitations _(if any)_:

_____

_____

_____

_____

_____

Special Collections Responsibilities

The materials shall be preserved, organized, and made available for research in accordance with Albion College Special Collections access and use policies. At any time hereafter, the donor shall be permitted to examine any of the materials upon making an appointment with the College Archivist.

Albion College is authorized to display any donated materials in non-profit exhibitions both on and off campus. Materials may be used to illustrate exhibition catalogs and College publications.

Albion College is authorized to dispose of any duplicate or inappropriate material in the collection that it determines has no permanent value or historical interest. The College is also authorized to sell, trade or dispose of any material in the collection that does not fit the collecting parameters of the Special Collections unit. If so desired, such materials as specified will be returned to the Donor.

Additions to the Collection

In the event that the Donor may hereafter donate additional materials to Albion College, such gifts will be governed by the terms and conditions stated above. A description of the additional materials so donated shall be prepared and attached hereto.

Tax Deduction Information

Appraised Value *(If the Donor has had the gift appraised)* _____

*Please attach a copy of the independent appraisal if available

If you do not intend to take a tax deduction, please initial here _____

Acceptance of Terms & Conditions

Donor

I represent and warrant that I am the sole owner of the materials described above and that I have full right, power and authority to give the materials mentioned above to Albion College. I have received a copy of this **Deed of Gift** and agree to all terms and conditions as stated, indicated by my signature below.

If applicable, I understand the sections on copyright and acknowledge that the information I have provided is accurate.

Signature _____

Date _____

Address _____

Telephone _____

Albion College Representative

The Special Collections unit, on behalf of Albion College, gratefully acknowledges receipt of this gift and agrees to the stipulations outlined above.

Signature _____

Date _____

Stockwell-Mudd Libraries Special Collections, Albion College, 602 E. Cass Street, Albion, MI 49224 | 517.629.0487 | archives@albion.edu

Albion College ∘ Albion, Michigan ∘ 517/629-1000
Home | Site Index | People Directory | Search | Contact Us
© 2004 All rights reserved.

Davidson College

DEED OF GIFT AGREEMENT
DAVIDSON COLLEGE LIBRARY
P.O. BOX 1837
DAVIDSON, NC 28036
(704) 892-2632

I, _____ (hereinafter referred to as the Donor), hereby give, donate, and convey to the Davidson College Library for the College Archives, the property, including any future additions to it, which is described in Appendix A, attached hereto.

Title and Transfer Provisions

1. Property Rights: Upon transfer to Davidson College the property is granted irrevocably and absolutely to the Davidson College Library.
    Any part of the property that is not retained by Davidson College shall be returned to the Donor, unless the Donor declines this offer as part of the deed agreement   Decline_____

2. Copyrights: Any copyrights such as the Donor may possess in this property are hereby dedicated to Davidson College.
    In the event that Davidson College would wish to deaccession the above described property, the Donor will have rights of first refusal and all property and literary rights would revert back to the Donor. unless the Donor declines this right as part of the deed of agreement.   Decline_____

Access

1. The Davidson College Archives will make this property available to research in accordance with standard archival procedures.

In full accord with the provisions of this deed of gift, I hereunto set my hand.

_____   _____
Legal Agent/Donor   Date

The foregoing gift of property is accepted on behalf of the Davidson College Library for the College Archives, subject to the terms and conditions heretofore set forth .

_____   _____
Library Director   Date

_____   _____
Davidson College Archivist   Date

Attached to and forming part of the instrument of gift of papers and other historical materials, executed by
_____ (Donor) on _____
and accepted by the Davidson College Library for the College Archives on _____.

Description of Property and any accompanying restrictions on access or use:

Eastern Washington University

EASTERN
Eastern Washington University
Cheney - Spokane

EXPLANATION OF DEED OF GIFT

The "Deed of Gift" is designed to legally assign to Eastern Washington University the collection of personal papers, corporate records or other materials which you as a Donor are placing here for care and administration. Besides expediting the transfer of title to the papers, the form also serves to define the terms of the transfer.

It has previously been the practice of many archival repositories to rely on correspondence with donors to substantiate donations and the conditions under which they were received. On recommendation of major organizations concerned with archival administration -- the Society of American Archivists, the American Library Association, and the Association of College and Research Libraries -- many repositories have adopted the use of a Deed of Gift or similar formal agreement to accomplish transfer of legal title.

Donation of Gift. The "Description" portion of this section will be completed by the representative of the University Archives. The "Description" of the donation will state the type of material transferred.

Access Restrictions. Though most Donors will have no need to limit access to collections of personal papers which they possess (especially if the papers relate to activities occurring several years in the past) the option of placing restrictions on access to a collection or a portion of a collection is always available to a Donor. A person may feel that portions of his / her papers contain records which are still too sensitive to allow access to such materials. That being the case, he / she may wish to specify a time period in which these records may not be used. This type of condition should be stated in the appropriate space on the Deed of Gift.

Single Copies. The privilege of ordering facsimiles (usually photocopies) is offered as a convenience to researchers, particularly to those who visit from great distances and whose time is limited. This practice is standard in the archival field. When copies are requested, researchers are informed that they may not quote for publication without permission.

Assignment of Literary Rights. To enable scholars to quote readily from papers, we encourage Donors to transfer literary rights which they possess to Eastern Washington University whenever possible. Unpublished writings created prior to December 31, 1977 are protected by copyright until at least January 1, 2003. For writings created after January 1, 1978, copyright protection extends for the life of the author plus 50 years. If the author's death date is not known, or of the author is unidentified, the writing is protected by copyright for 100 years following its creation. Assignment of literary rights may be effected with specific limitations. A Donor may wish to stipulate, "Literary rights retained during my life-time," or something similar in the section for Limiting Conditions.

Distribution and Disposition of Materials. In order to insure maximum use of a donation of personal papers, and in order to best utilize library resources, the Archives & Special Collections reserves the right to distribute and dispose of materials contained in a collection as it deems most suitable. Examples of materials often judged to be inappropriate for care and attention by the Archives are: books, periodicals, multiple copies, and published maps. Materials such as books and periodicals are normally routed to other library units where they can be more appropriately housed and cared for. Ephemeral material and pamphlets are often routed to the vertical file, and maps to the map collection. Multiple copies and materials which will not fit into library collections can most often be disposed of without in any way impairing the value of a collection. If the Donor wishes any duplicate materials or materials not wanted by the Library returned, she / he should check the appropriate statement on the Deed of Gift.

Acknowledgement of Gift. The Archives & Special Collections Department, on behalf of Eastern Washington University, gratefully acknowledges your gift. Your donation of materials is sincerely appreciated as an important addition to the Collections.

Eastern Washington University Libraries
Archives & Special collections
100 LIB - 816 F Street
Cheney, Washington 99004-2453
Telephone (509) 359-2475 * FAX (509) 359-6456 * email cmutschler@ewu.edu

156 Deed of Gift Forms

EASTERN

Eastern Washington University
Cheney - Spokane

DEED OF GIFT

The following collection is herewith presented as a gift to Eastern Washington University, with the understanding that it shall be cared for in a manner which will, in the judgment of the University, best provide for its physical preservation and at the same time make it most readily available to persons qualified to use manuscripts and records in the University Archives and Special Collections.

Description of the collection:

Consists of the[personal papers or records – use the appropriate term] of [_Name of donor] . These document [insert brief description of the scope and content of the records]. See detailed list accompanying this document for list of materials received.

The collection described above was received by:

_____   _____
Date   Eastern Washington University Representative

I/we give this property to Eastern Washington University as an unrestricted gift and relinquish any literary rights that I/we may possess to contents unless limiting conditions are specifically stated herein:

Some series and file folders are closed, pursuant to the wishes of the donor. Permission to use this collection does not constitute permission to quote or publish from these papers. The donor retains specific rights to publish from his [use her if donor is female] research, and to restrict access to his papers during his lifetime. These are spelled out in the accompanying letter on limiting conditions.

( )   I agree that any materials in the collection described felt to be inappropriate to the Archives & Special Collections or the general collection shall be disposed of by the Archives as it sees fit.

( )   Any such materials shall be returned to me/us.

_____   _____
Date   Signature of Donor

_____   _____
Date   Signature of Donor

                         Printed Name_____

                         Address_____

                         _____

Eastern Washington University Libraries
Archives & Special Collections
100 LIB - 816 F Street
Cheney, Washington 99004-2453
Telephone (509) 359-2475 * FAX (509) 359-6456 *email charles.mutschler@mailserver.ewu.edu

Deed of Gift Forms 157

RAUGUST LIBRARY ARCHIVES

STATEMENT OF GIFT

I own the materials described below and voluntarily donate them to Raugust Library, Jamestown College. The date of the transfer will be at my death or at an earlier time mutually agreed upon by me and Jamestown College. It is understood that the purpose and intent of this gift is to transfer and assign all rights, title and interest I possess to these materials to the Library, except as specified below. Raugust Library may use its discretion to dispose of material inappropriate for its collections, unless instructions to return unwanted materials to the donor are stated below.

Description of materials:

Restrictions on the use of and/or access to these materials:

_____   _____
Signature of donor or agent   Date

_____   _____
Signature of Library representative Date

Donor:

Address:

Telephone:

Accession numbers:

6000 College Lane • Jamestown, ND 58405 • Tel: (701) 252-3467 • Fax: (701) 253-4318

SOUTH CAROLINIANA LIBRARY
THE UNIVERSITY OF SOUTH CAROLINA
COLUMBIA, SOUTH CAROLINA 29208

DECLARATION OF GIFT AND
ACKNOWLEDGEMENT OF RECEIPT

The South Caroliniana Library gratefully accepts from:

Name of Donor or Agent   : _____

Address   : _____
   _____

the following materials:

The Donor(s) assigns and conveys to The University of South Carolina, for the use of the South Caroliniana Library, all legal title, property and copyright to the materials described above (and any future additions), and any literary property rights which The Donor(s) possesses to the contents of any of the donor's letters or writings in other colections of The South Caroliniana Library unless limiting conditions are specifically stated as follows:

It is further agreed and understood that The South Caroliniana Library shall incur no financial encumbrances of any kind with this gift.

Items not retained by The South Caroliniana Library shall be:

[ ] disposed of at the discretion of The South Caroliniana Library (including transfer to other repositories)
[ ] returned to the donor
[ ] other, describe:

This form constitutes a full agreement by and between the undersigned parties. No amendments, deletions or modifications to this agreement shall be valid unless stated in writing and signed by the undersigned parties. Final approval of all gifts is with the Director of The South Caroliniana Library.

_____   _____
Signature of Donee   Signature of Donor(s)

_____   _____
Date   Date

Deed of Gift Forms 159

WILLIAMS COLLEGE ARCHIVES AND SPECIAL COLLECTIONS

EXPLANATION OF THE DEED OF GIFT

The enclosed Deed of Gift form is designed to legally assign to the Williams College Library a collection of personal papers or other materials which you as a Donor are placing here for care and administration. Besides expediting the transfer of title to the papers, the Deed of Gift form also serves to define the terms of the transfer.

DONATION OF GIFT. The 'Name' and 'Description' portions of this section will be completed by the Library. The 'Description' of the donation will state the type of material transferred.

ACCESS RESTRICTIONS. Although most Donors will have no need to limit access to collections of personal papers which they possess (especially if the papers relate to activities occurring several years in the past), the option of placing restrictions on access to a collection or portion of a collection is always available to a Donor.

ASSIGNMENT OF LITERARY RIGHTS. To enable scholars to quote readily from papers, we encourage Donors to transfer literary rights which they possess to Williams College whenever possible.

It should be noted that conveyance of literary rights applies only to communications of the person who actually created the papers and for whom they are named. Literary rights to writings of other individuals and organizations contained in the personal papers remain with those individuals and organizations and cannot be transferred by the Donor; only physical property in those writings is transferred.

GIFT OF
THE PAPERS OF

Name of individual or family

TO THE WILLIAMS COLLEGE LIBRARY
WILLIAMSTOWN, MASSACHUSETTS

I, _____ (hereinafter referred to as the Donor), hereby give, donate and convey to Williams College for deposit in the Williams College Library and for administration therein by the authorities thereof the following papers (listing attached). The gift of these papers, and of papers and materials that I may from time to time send to Williams College in the future, is made subject to the following terms and conditions:

1. Title to the papers and other materials transferred hereunder will pass to Williams College as of the date of the signing of this instrument.

2. It is the Donor's wish that the papers and other materials donated to the Williams College Library by the terms of this instrument be made available for research in the Williams College Library as soon as they have been received, arranged and cataloged. The papers shall be made available for research purposes in accordance with the regulations and policies of the Williams College Library governing the use of manuscript materials for research purposes.

3. The Donor hereby gives, donates and conveys to Williams College all literary and other property rights in the unpublished letters and other manuscripts that have hereby been given or that may later be given to the Williams College Library.

Signed _____

Date _____

****

Accepted _____

Date _____

RECORDS TRANSFER POLICIES AND FORMS

Bowdoin College Archives -- RECORDS TRANSMITTAL FORM

PART 1 - To be completed by transferring department			
Department / Office			
Name of contact person			Ext:
Physical type of documents (files, volumes, posters, videos, etc.)			
Number of pieces	Boxes:	Volumes:	Other:
Dimensions of pieces (volume or linear footage, please specify)	Boxes:	Volumes:	Other:
Physical condition / special care instructions	Boxes:	Volumes:	Other:
Indexes or registers available			
Other remarks (e.g. origin of documents if not created by the department; purpose or subject matter of documents, special instructions, etc.):			
Method of transfer (e.g. hand-carried, campus mail, facilities management work order)			

Transferred by:	Received by:
Signature:	Signature:
Date of transfer:	Date of receipt:

PART 2 - To be completed by Archives staff
DISPOSITION:

Destruction date (if applicable):	**Accession Number:**

Ohio Northern University

Heterick Memorial Library
Ohio Northern University

Section I: Statement of Purpose and Mission

This policy is established to issue general guidelines, procedures, and suggestions for the permanent preservation of Ohio Northern University records of enduring historical and administrative value; and for achieving economy and efficiency in the creation, maintenance, use, and disposition of University records. This policy is intended first and foremost to protect the privacy of all living individuals associated with the University, as well as their immediate families. It is also intended to facilitate legitimate historical research once privacy rights are no longer operative. The guidelines established in this policy will adhere to the Family Educational Rights and Privacy Act of 1974 and its revisions.

The Ohio Northern University Archives, exists as a repository for all non-current, inactive official records of all University administrative offices and academic departments. The Archives will collect, preserve, and maintain such records regardless of format to chronicle the historical development of the University; and protect and make these records available to University offices and departments, students, and scholars to aid in research on the history of the institution and on the development of academic disciplines.

In addition to collecting, storing, and maintaining official University records, the Archives will assist with the procurement of non-official and non-University manuscript and pertinent archival collections that enhance and contribute to the University's various academic, technical, and technological areas of study and interest. It will be within the University's policy to focus collections in areas which are logical extensions of the research strengths, interests, and needs of the University faculty, and that anticipate future research needs; in fields where the Heterick Memorial Library has extensive holdings of published materials; and where there is a high ratio of use to volume and processing costs. It will not be the University's policy to directly compete with major collectors in the region.

The guidelines established for non-official and non-University records are not considered mandatory; but, instead, are formulated for consideration in the donation and acquisition of such records into the Archives.

'' A Project of the librarians of Heterick Memorial Library
Please send questions or comments to : i-canagaratna@onu.edu
Heterick Memorial Library - Ohio Northern University - 525 S. Main Street - Ada, OH-45810
Telephone : (419) 772-2181 Fax: (419) 772-1927

Ohio Northern University

Section II: Organizational and Administrative Practices and Procedures of the University Archives

The University Archives, established by administrative declaration, is a department of the Heterick Memorial Library. The University Archivist is directly responsible to the Library Director. All operational decisions for the Archives will be consistent with the policies and procedures of the Library.

The Archivist works directly with University administrative offices and academic departments to assure the on-going fulfillment of the purposes and mission of the Archives. The Archivist has discretion concerning the transfer and disposal of all official University records. Policies and procedures approved by the Administration will be followed. The archives program will follow, where appropriate and when possible, the Guidelines for College & University Archives, published by the Society of American Archivists.

There shall be a central repository where archival records and associated material will be stored and made available for research. This area shall be secure, subject to temperature and humidity control, and have a fire suppression system installed. Other repositories and areas may be utilized for the retention and use of archival collections deemed non-Official. All such areas are subject to the review of the Archivist.

The University embraces the principle of "openness" and seeks to provide maximum access to its records commensurate with the efficient operation of the University. As such, and in general, the Archives will meet reasonable requests for access to information without the need for application under the Freedom of Information Act of 1992 and its revisions. For security purposes, the granting of access to the Archives will be the responsibility of the Archivist or whomsoever is acting in the capacity of the Archivist; and in accordance with the originating or transferring agency where applicable.

It shall be the responsibility of the Archivist to formulate a standard procedure for the disposal of official University records; and to approve and witness the disposal of such records. The Archivist will record the date and time of disposal, and keep a permanent copy of the disposal list of contents. Where federal and state laws govern the disposal of records, these laws will supersede any applicable guidelines outlined in this policy. In all instances, the Archivist should be apprised of the federal and state laws governing the retention and disposal of any University records.

The President will appoint members to an Archives and Records Management Committee; which will advise on matters of archival policy and practice, and the formulation and implementation of a records management program. The Committee will periodically review the University Archives Policy and recommend amendments to the President.

" A Project of the librarians of Heterick Memorial Library
Please send questions or comments to : i-canagaratna@onu.edu
Heterick Memorial Library - Ohio Northern University - 525 S. Main Street - Ada, OH-45810

Ohio Northern University

Section III: Guidelines for Office Records of Campus Administrative and Academic Departments

Official University records are considered all documentary materials, regardless of physical medium or characteristics, generated or received by the various administrative offices and academic departments of the University in the conduct of their business, regardless of the form in which they are created and maintained. Such records are considered the property of the University and constitute archival material. Consequently, archival material consists of documents containing historical evidence or any records containing evidence and information about the University's history, organization, function, and structure. The Archives thus constitutes the official memory of the University and represents the accumulated experience of its members.

Non-official records are considered all documentary materials, regardless of physical medium or characteristics, that are not necessarily generated by or at the University, yet enhance and contribute to the University's various academic, technical, and technological areas of study and interest.

Records commonly transferred to the Archives include:

1. Constitutions and by-laws, minutes and proceedings, transcripts, lists of officers of University corporate bodies;

2. Office Files: correspondence and memoranda (incoming and outgoing) and subject files concerning projects, activities, and functions;

3. Financial records reflecting the status of University funds, including but not restricted to annual budget submissions, annual financial statements, and general ledger reports;

4. Historical files documenting policies, decisions, committee and task force reports, and questionnaires;

5. Publications: one record copy of all newsletters, brochures, journals, monographs, programs, posters, and announcements issued by the University or its subdivisions. The Archives should be placed on University, departmental, and office mailing lists to receive all publications;

6. Audio-Visuals: photographs and negatives, maps, plans, films, sound and video recordings, microforms, and miscellaneous media depicting general university life;

7. Reports of external bodies about University operations, accreditation, audits, etc.;

8. Academic program materials: curricula, feasibility studies, and class schedules;

9. Records and minutes of student organizations and University-sponsored associations, including social and civic groups;

10. Artifacts and memorabilia: material of significance to the history of the University and manageable in physical size and condition.

Note: All information formats (e.g. published, typescript, audio-visual, and electronic data such as computer disks and files) are appropriate for consideration for transfer. For documents in formats requiring any form of machine intervention, such as videotapes, kinescopes, etc., and all computer files, consideration should be given for transferring the equipment needed to access the

Ohio Northern University

documents or, preferably, converting the documents to a format accessible to the Archives' users. Early consultation with the Archivist is strongly recommended for all such materials.

Records which generally should not be transferred to the Archives, but schedule for disposal after consultation with the Archivist include:

1. Records of specific financial transactions;

2. Routine correspondence of transmittal and acknowledgment;

3. Non-personally addressed correspondence such as memoranda (except for one record copy from the issuing officer);

4. General administrative and management files;

5. Student academic and employment records;

6. Requests for publications or information after the requests have been filed;

7. Replies to questionnaires if the results are recorded and preserved either in the Archives or in a published report.

Items which may be discarded directly from the office when they are no longer needed for administrative purposes include:

1. All blank forms and unused printed or duplicated material;

2. All other duplicate material: keep only the original and annotated copies; 3. Papers, reports, working papers, and drafts which have been published;

4. Miscellaneous candid visual and audio materials.

Note: This list is intended as a general guide. If there are questions about records or other material not listed here or questions about the retention and disposal of specific records, please contact the Archivist.

`` A Project of the librarians of Heterick Memorial Library
Please send questions or comments to : i-canagaratna@onu.edu
Heterick Memorial Library - Ohio Northern University - 525 S. Main Street - Ada, OH-45810
Telephone : (419) 772-2181 Fax: (419) 772-1927

Section IV: Guidelines for Personal Papers of Faculty and Staff

Ohio Northern University is the repository of not only the non-current records of the University, but also the personal papers of faculty and staff. The Archives will endeavor to collect and maintain these records for their intrinsic value in documenting the history of the institution and on the development of academic disciplines. It is recognized that the personal papers of faculty and staff constitute a rich source for historical research. Such records are considered non-official records. The following guidelines will assist faculty and staff in identifying those portions of their files that are appropriate for transfer to the Archives.

Items likely to be of archival interest include:

1. Biographical information: resumes and published and unpublished biographical sketches;

2. University official correspondence and files: outgoing and incoming letters and memoranda relating to departmental and University business, committee minutes, reports, and files;

3. Professional correspondence (outgoing and incoming) with colleagues, publishers, professional organizations, and former students;

4. Teaching material: one copy of lecture notes, syllabi, course outlines, reading lists, examinations, and correspondence with students;

5. Publications: one copy of all articles, books, reviews or works of art and other professional construction;

6. Audio-Visuals: photographs, films, and sound and video recordings;

7. Personal and family correspondence, diaries, and photographs.

Note: All information formats (e.g. published, typescript, audio-visual, and electronic data such as computer disks and files) are appropriate for consideration for transfer. For documents in formats requiring any for of machine intervention, such as videotapes, kinescopes, etc., and all computer files, consideration should be given to transferring the equipment needed to access the documents or images or, preferably, converting the documents or images to a format accessible to the Archives' users. Early consultation with the Archivist is strongly encouraged for all such materials.

Documents which generally should not be transferred without prior consultation with the Archivist include:

1. Detailed financial records, canceled checks, and receipts;

2. Routine correspondence, especially non-personally addressed mail and routine letters of transmittal and acknowledgment;

3. Grade books and class rosters;

4. Duplicates and multiple copies of publications and course materials;

5. Typescripts, drafts, and galleys of publications and speeches unless the final publication or presentation is unavailable;

6. Books, research papers, journal articles, and reprints written by other persons (unless its significance will be lost if destroyed);

7. Research notes and data if a summary of the data is available and transferred; bibliographic notes and notes on reading (unless its significance will be lost if destroyed);

8. Artifacts and memorabilia: Material of significance and approved by the Archivist will be considered; and, in manageable physical size and condition

" A Project of the librarians of Heterick Memorial Library
Please send questions or comments to : i-canagaratna@onu.edu
Heterick Memorial Library - Ohio Northern University - 525 S. Main Street - Ada, OH-45810
Telephone : (419) 772-2181 Fax: (419) 772-1927

Section V: Guidelines for Personal Papers of Alumni and Others

Ohio Northern University will seek to obtain both the non-current records of the University and the personal papers of faculty, staff, alumni, former students, and others associated with the University. Manuscript and archival collections documenting the post-University careers of alumni are actively collected to provide documentation that supports the research interests and needs of faculty and students and to strengthen holdings in subject areas of the University. Collecting and preserving such records provide important insights into the history of the University and can provide a basis for research in broad areas of American life and culture. Such records are considered non-official records. The following guidelines are intended to assist donors of such records, and their families, in identifying those portions of their files that are appropriate for transfer to the University.

Items likely to be of archival interest include:

1. Biographical information: resumes, bibliographies, memoirs, genealogies, and published and manuscript biographical sketches;

2. Ohio Northern University correspondence and files: outgoing and incoming correspondence, diaries, photographs and negatives, and scrapbooks that provide documentation of university experience relating to enrollment, attendance, involvement in student and alumni organizations and activities;

3. Professional correspondence (outgoing and incoming) with business associates, colleagues, and professional organizations;

4. Personal correspondence with Ohio Northern University alumni and students;

5. Course material: class notebooks, student papers, exams, and correspondence relating to the academic career at Ohio Northern University;

6. Publications: one copy of all articles, books, reviews or works of art and other professional construction;

7. Audio-Visuals: photographs, films, and sound and video recordings;

8. Family correspondence, diaries, photographs, and financial, legal, and technical documents, except where there is family interest in retaining and preserving such materials;

9. Summary financial records where relevant to business and career activities documented elsewhere in the records;

10. Organizational records and correspondence relating to membership and participation in professional, civic, and social associations and organizations.

Note: All information formats (e.g. published, typescript, audio-visual, and electronic data such as computer disks and files) are appropriate for consideration and acceptance. For documents in formats requiring any form of machine intervention, such as videotapes, kinescopes, etc., and all computer files, consideration should be given to donating the equipment needed to access the documents or, preferably, converting them to an accessible format. Consultation with the ONU Archivist is strongly recommended for all such materials.

Documents which generally should not be donated or transferred without prior consultation with the ONU Archivist are similar to those outlined for the faculty and staff in the previous section.

`` A Project of the librarians of Heterick Memorial Library
Please send questions or comments to : i-canagaratna@onu.edu
Heterick Memorial Library - Ohio Northern University - 525 S. Main Street - Ada, OH-45810
Telephone : (419) 772-2181 Fax: (419) 772-1927

Ohio Northern University

Heterick Memorial Library
Ohio Northern University

Contact Us
Library Hours

ONU Home   Library Home   Arts & Sciences   Business   Engineering   Pharmacy   Law

Section VI: Guidelines for Records of Educational and Professional Associations

Items likely to be of archival interest include:

1. Official records: constitutions and by-laws, minutes and proceedings, transcripts, and lists of officers and members; financial reports;

2. Office files: correspondence and memoranda (incoming and outgoing) and subject files concerning projects, activities, and functions;

3. Historical files documenting policies and decisions, committee and task force reports, and questionnaires; successful grant applications;

4. Publications: one record copy of all programs, journals, monographs, newsletters, brochures, announcements, media , posters and other ephemeral material created and issued by the association and its subdivisions;

5. Audio-Visuals: photographs and negatives, films, and sound recordings;

6. Personal papers of members which relate directly to association work;

7. Charts, maps, and other association graphics.

Items not considered significant for archival preservation include:releases

1. Records of specific financial and membership transactions;

2. Requests for publications or information after the requests have been filed;

3. All blank forms and unused printed or duplicated material;

4. All duplicate material;

5. Papers, reports, work papers and drafts which have been published;

6. Replies to questionnaires if the results are recorded and preserved in a published report.

`` A Project of the librarians of Heterick Memorial Library
Please send questions or comments to : i-canagaratna@onu.edu
Heterick Memorial Library - Ohio Northern University - 525 S. Main Street - Ada, OH-45810
Telephone : (419) 772-2181 Fax: (419) 772-1927

Heterick Memorial Library
Ohio Northern University

ONU Home   Library Home   Arts & Sciences   Business   Engineering   Pharmacy   Law

Section VII: The Transfer and Disposal of Records

While the Archives serves as the repository for all official records of the University, it may serve as the repository of non-University manuscript and pertinent archival collections. In certain instances, subject to the approval of the President of the University, such records may be kept and maintained within specific academic departments for ongoing research use, and reviewed for safety and security by the Archivist. In no instance will official University records be kept and maintained in this manner.

All materials transferred to the Archives should be done in the order in which the creator of the records maintained them. A Transfer Form obtainable from the Archivist, briefly identifying the materials and describing the activity to which it relates, should accompany the transfer. All transfers should be arranged with the Archivist in advance of the transfer.

The lists of guidelines established in this policy are intended as general rules. If there are questions about the retention or disposal of specific records, the Archivist should be contacted or informed.

Transferring Records:

All material no longer needed in the office in which it originated will be subject for either transfer to the Archives or disposed. No items will be moved, however, until the Archives is prepared to receive it. The administrative head of the office or the chair of the academic department, in consultation with the Archivist, should establish a time and date to schedule the transfer of any records. Documents should be kept in their original folders and should be packed for transfer according to the filing system employed in the respective office. A filing list of the records should be sent with the material. The person responsible for the transfer should consult with the Archivist before assembling the material; and arrange for the Archivist or the Archivist's designee to be present when the files are packed for transfer to prevent any uncertainty when reassembling the material in the Archives.

Disposing of Records:

In like manner, the Archivist should be notified of any records not governed by federal or state laws deemed ready for disposal. The Archivist will arrange with the respective administrative head or academic chair for the disposal of the records at a mutually agreed upon time and date. All University records approved and eligible for destruction must be destroyed under confidential conditions, unless the material is widely published and accessible to the general public.

All records transferred to the Archives or disposed by consent of the Archivist should be reported to the Archives and Records Management Committee at the earliest date following action.

" A Project of the librarians of Heterick Memorial Library
Please send questions or comments to : i-canagaratna@onu.edu
Heterick Memorial Library - Ohio Northern University - 525 S. Main Street - Ada, OH-45810
Telephone : (419) 772-2181 Fax: (419) 772-1927

CATALOGING PROCEDURES

III. Classification

The latest edition of the Dewey Decimal Classification tables, found online at http://connexion.oclc.org/ is used to classify, with some qualifications and exceptions. The Library accepts the Phoenix tables, the number expansions and other changes in each successive edition of Dewey with reasonably good grace. Expansion of numbers is generally not a problem and is usually welcome. Major changes in each new edition of the tables are noted and weeding/reclassification projects are planned when time permits.

With the advent of each new edition of Dewey, decisions are made concerning local applications of changes, and these decisions are recorded in the tables themselves. To ensure continuity, each new edition must be checked against the last and linear notes and past decisions transferred from the old to the new. Some linear notes have been made to the online version of *Dewey.*

The suggested Dewey number found in the book as part of the Cataloging-in-Publication (CIP) data or on an LC-generated OCLC record can usually be accepted by the library, but each number must be examined for accuracy, currency and conformity to our own practices. As with the application of subject headings, common sense on the part of the cataloger is crucial when it comes to number-building. In current practice, numbers are expanded to suit the present needs of the collection but with an eye to future needs also. In number-building the curriculum of the college must be a major consideration.

When in doubt about the acceptability of a suggested number, shelflist the III database and search for similar Dewey numbers by typing "c" and then the entire number. To verify local numbers, use "l" [el] and then the Cutter number.

> ex. c821.7 K25   -- will bring up the shelflist on John Keats
> l A123k   -- will search the juvenile, Pa. German shelflist

****

4. Rare Book Collection

This collection was previously called the Treasure collection, hence the prestamp T. This collection includes first editions, autographed copies, valuable editions, examples of fine printing, etc. Most of this collection has been transferred from the main circulating collection or has been received as gifts. A general guideline has been to put all pre-1850 American imprints and all pre-1800 foreign imprints into this collection. All pre-1830, German language American imprints, however, should be placed in the Pennsylvania German Collection.

The collection is housed in the Special Collections area to the right of the Exhibit Room and is classified the same as the main circulating collection. The call number is prefaced by the letter T. Materials in this collection do not circulate.

Some amount of special handling by the cataloger is required for Rare Books. They are not barcoded, targeted, or stamped in any way. A bookplate is pasted on the front right flyleaf and a strip of acid-free, tabbed paper is placed in the book giving the call number, author and a short title. A barcode is attached to the back of this strip.

For more information on the contents of and the circulation procedures for the Rare Book Collection see Appendix A, Special Collections Access Policy and Procedure Guide.

5. Pennsylvania German Collection

The Pennsylvania German Collection contains print and non-print materials that pertain to the history, social customs and language of the early German immigrants to Pennsylvania. Also, the collection contains pre-1830 German language American imprints, as well as some local history, church history and genealogical materials. The emphasis has been on collecting materials about the early German settlers in Lehigh, Northampton, Bucks, and Montgomery counties rather than in other geographical areas of Pennsylvania that are covered in other Pennsylvania German collections at Millersville University, Franklin and Marshall College, Ursinus College and Penn State.

Materials in this collection do not circulate. It has been the library's policy to purchase two copies of titles selected for the

P.G. Collection--one for the circulating collection and one for the special collection.

Post-1830 material does get stamped, barcoded and targeted; pre-1830 materials receive the same treatment as rare books. They are not barcoded, targeted or stamped in any way. A bookplate is pasted on the front, right flyleaf and a strip of acid-free tabbed paper is placed in the book giving the call number, author and a short title; a barcode is attached to the back of the strip.

The collection is housed in the Special Collections area off the Exhibit Room on Level B. Prior to 1998, Materials were assigned a Cutter number based on the main entry, generally, which is prefaced by the letters P.G. In 2000, the collection was reclassified into Dewey numbers.

> P.G.
> 974.800431
> K63p   Klees. The Pennsylvania Dutch.

Church histories are classified with the denominations in the Dewey 200s and cuttered by the community in which the church resides. AACR stated that a local church should be entered under the name of the place in which it is located and this rule is still valid for this collection. Work marks are taken from the name of the church.

> P.G.
> 284.174816
> T657t   Topton, Pa. Trinity Lutheran Church.
>   Fifty years.

County churches, however, located in a county with no community attachments, are entered by the distinctive church name followed by the county name. These histories are cuttered by the church name.

> P.G.
> 284.174827
> Z663o   Ziegel's Church, Lehigh County,   Pa.
>   175th anniversary of the dedication...

Family histories are classified in Dewey 929.2 and cuttered by the family name. Work marks are taken from the author or editor.

> P.G.
> 929.2
> W4272r   Richards.   The Weiser family.

For more information on the contents of and circulation procedures for the Pennsylvania German Collection see Appendix A, <u>Special Collections Access Policy and Procedure Guide</u>.

6. Muhlenberg College Collection

The Muhlenberg College Collection contains print and non-print material relating to the college, including college, faculty, student and alumni publications.

The collection is housed in the Special Collections area to the right of the Exhibit Room on Level B. Materials in this collection do not circulate.

It is the library's policy to purchase two copies of titles selected for the Muhlenberg College Collection--one for the circulating collection and one for the special collection. This policy is also true for some college and student publications -- if two copies are available, a circulating copy is introduced.

Books and other materials are classified according to the table reproduced below. Faculty, alumni and students publications are cuttered by the author's name. The call number is prefaced by the letters M.C.

> M.C.
> M
> M888c
> 1983   Mortimer.   Chemistry.

Publications by and about the college are classed according to the issuing body and cuttered M952-. The work mark is taken from either the title or from the office issuing the document.

        M.C.
        N
        M952<u>mi</u>   Muhlenberg College.
                        Minute book of the faculty.
        M.C.
        R
        M952<u>s</u>   Muhlenberg College. Sophronian Society.
                        (Records) (Manuscript)

While the Muhlenberg College Collection is not the official archives of the college, some committee minutes, annual reports, policy statements and memorabilia, etc. are housed in filing cabinets and called "ephemera" for what of a better term. The arrangement of this collection is based on a locally modified **Table for College and University Publications** which was found in the DDC, 18th ed.

        A Charter and Statutes
        B Trustees
        C Office of the President
        D Administrative Offices
        E History
        F Memorabilia
        G Calendars
        H   Programs and events
        I   Guest speakers
        J Curriculum
        K Evening College/Summer School/Continuing
                Education Program
        L Academic Departments
        M Faculty Publications
        N Faculty Committee Minutes, including Faculty
                Meeting
        O Inter-collegiate sports
        P Greek Societies
        Q Student Publications
        R Student Organizations
        S Student Activities
        T Alumni Publications

U   Alumni Activities
V   Open
W   Buildings and Grounds
X   Open
Y   Campus Endeavors/Campus Outreach Programs
Z   Associate Organizations

A complete, up-to-date list of the files held is kept on top of the filing cabinets and in the Special Collections notebook at the Reference Desk. The master list is kept with the Special Collections Librarian.

For more information on the contents of and circulation procedures for the Muhlenberg Collection, see Appendix A, Special Collections Access Policy and Procedure Guide.

7. Brennan Map Collection

The Ray R. Brennan Map Collection includes both books on the history of cartography, atlases and maps, many dating to the 17th and 18th century. Many of the large maps are framed and have been placed on Levels B and C of the Library with suitable donor plaques. The books and atlases have been classified and cuttered according to the rules adapted for the Main Collection. They are not barcoded, targeted or stamped in any way. A bookplate is pasted on the front, right flyleaf and a strip of acid-free tabbed paper is placed in the book giving the call number, author and a short title; a barcode is attached to the back of the strip These materials are housed in the steel display case in the Special Collections storage area off the Exhibit Room.

The maps, both framed and unframed have been arranged in general geographical divisions, ex. WO for world maps, PA for Pennsylvania maps, NA for maps of North America, and assigned a consecutive accession number, within the category. Maps in frames have targets, barcodes, ownership labels and call number labels on the back of the frames. Unframed maps have been carefully stamped for ownership on the verso.and placed in acid-free, letter-sized manilla folders. Call number labels are affixed to the folders. The folders assist in handling the materials. Unframed maps are

stored in the map case in Special Collections; the framed
maps have been hung on the walls in the Special Collections
storage area. All materials have the prestamp B.C.

B.C.
WO 1   Homan.   Planiglobii terrestris …

For more information on the Ray R. Brennan Map Collection see the
<u>Guide to the Ray R. Brennan Map Collection.</u>

REQUEST TO PUBLISH POLICIES AND FORMS

BUTLER UNIVERSITY

Butler University

4600 Sunset Avenue
Indianapolis, Indiana 46208-3485
OFFICE: (317) 940-9227
FAX: (317) 940-9711

PERMISSION TO PUBLISH CONTRACT

Author/Presenter_____ Telephone (   )_____

Address_____ Fax (   )_____

_____ E-mail_____

Publisher/Venue_____

Address_____

_____

_____

Title of Publication/Presentation/Exhibition, etc._____

Projected date of completion_____

Items from the collection of the Butler University Libraries Special Collections, Rare Books, and University Archives division to be used in the above publication/presentation/ exhibition (cite specifically by collection name and shelflist number, call number, and date of document:_____

_____

_____

Permission to use the materials above is hereby granted, **provided:**

1. That written permission for the intended use is secured from the holder of copyright in the material when copyright is not held by Butler University.
2. That the author/presenter and/or publisher/sponsor assume(s) full and complete legal responsibility for any infringement of copyright that might occur from the use or publication of this material. The undersigned hereby indemnifies Butler University, its officers, and employees for any and all losses, costs, and legal fees that accrue to Butler University from failure of the undersigned to obtain appropriate permissions.
3. That full credit be given to Butler University Libraries as the source of the material. The credit line will read: "[Name and Number] Collection, Butler University Libraries."
4. That a copy of any publication or product resulting from the use of this material, including any publicity or related documentation, be given to Butler University Libraries for its documentary files.
5. That the completed project meets the commonly accepted standards of scholarship.

In order to secure permission to use or quote from sources for which Butler University does not hold copyright, the following information is provided:_____

_____

Failure to abide by the conditions of this contract may result in prosecution.

_____   _____
Signature of author/presenter/publisher/sponsor   Date

_____   _____
Signature for Butler University Libraries representative   Date

The Claremont Colleges

Special Collections, Honnold/Mudd Library
Claremont University Consortium

NOTIFICATION OF INTENT TO PUBLISH SPECIAL COLLECTIONS MATERIALS

Conditions of Publication of Special Collections Materials:

1. All requests will be considered on a case-by-case basis.
2. Special Collections will assess a use fee for the commercial publication of each item from its collection. Special Collections reserves the right to judge whether a proposed publication is commercial, based on the nature of the publication, the publisher, and the intended circulation. Special Collections also reserves the right to assess a use fee for a scholarly publication if it consists extensively or exclusively of materials from Special Collections.
3. Special Collections reserves the right to limit the number of items to be published.
4. Use fees cover non-exclusive, one time use of a single item unless otherwise indicated and are to be paid in advance of publication. Use fees are assessed in addition to any duplication costs. Rights are not granted in perpetuity. Images may not be archived.
5. Publication can take place only under the provisions of the fair use doctrine in the U.S. Copyright Law (as amended) or by obtaining permission of the copyright holder, which in some instances may be Special Collections, Honnold/Mudd Library, Claremont University Consortium.
6. Special Collections must be assured that the proposed publication will result in a suitable presentation of the original. Alteration of the original is prohibited.
7. No unauthorized copies may be made of the materials provided.
8. All publication of Special Collections materials must bear the credit line which must appear in conjunction with the reproduction:

   SPECIAL COLLECTIONS, HONNOLD/MUDD LIBRARY, CLAREMONT UNIVERSITY CONSORTIUM

9. Special Collections requests a complimentary copy of any publication, in any medium, that makes use of its materials be given to Special Collections for its collections.
10. THE APPLICANT WILL DEFEND, INDEMNIFY, AND HOLD HARMLESS SPECIAL COLLECTIONS AND CLAREMONT UNIVERSITY CONSORTIUM, ITS BOARD OF GOVERNORS, ITS OFFICERS, EMPLOYEES, AND AGENTS AGAINST ALL CLAIMS, DEMANDS, COSTS, AND EXPENSES INCLUDING ATTORNEYS' FEES INCURRED BY COPYRIGHT INFRINGEMENT OR ANY OTHER LEGAL OR REGULATORY COURSE OF ACTION ARISING FROM THE USE OF SPECIAL COLLECTIONS MATERIALS.

Agreement: I certify that the information provided herein is correct. Further, I have read, understand, and by my signature below, agree to abide by the rules, regulations, and obligations imposed upon me by Special Collections as set forth in "Conditions of Publication of Special Collections Materials" above.

Applicant signature: _____

Date: _____

10/02

Davidson College Archives
E. H. Little Library
P.O. Box 1837
Davidson, NC 28036

APPLICATION FOR PERMISSION TO REPRODUCE OR PUBLISH

Name of Applicant:_____
Organization or Agency (if appropriate):_____
Address:_____

MATERIAL TO BE REPRODUCED OR PUBLISHED
Title or description of item:

INTENDED USE OF MATERIAL
Title or description of use:

Publisher:
Projected date of publication:
Number of reproductions:
Size of edition/market:

CONDITIONS OF USE:

1. All requests to reproduce items from our holdings must be submitted on this application. By signing this application, the applicant agrees to abide by all conditions and provisions.

　　　Permission for reproduction is granted only when this application is countersigned by an authorized representative of the repository. Permission for reproduction is limited to the applicant and is non-transferable.

　　　Permission for reproduction is granted only for the purpose described in this application. This permission is non-exclusive; the repository reserves the right to reproduce the image and to allow others to reproduce the image.

　　　Any subsequent use (including subsequent editions, paperback editions, foreign language editions, electronic editions, etc.) constitutes reuse and must be applied for in writing to the repository.

　　　The repository reserves the right to refuse reproduction of its holdings if it feels fulfillment of that order would be in violation of copyright law or other law. The repository reserves the right to refuse reproduction of its holdings and to impose such conditions as it may deem advisable in the best interests of the repository.

2. In addition to the permission of the repository, additional permission may be required. Those

permissions may include, but are not limited to:

COPYRIGHT: The Davidson College Archives does not hold the copyright to items in its collection. If the work is subject to copyright, the copyright remains with the producer or publisher of the work or others to whom the copyright may have been assigned. The researcher is responsible for obtaining permission from the copyright holder before publishing any of this material.

> NOTICE
> WARNING CONCERNING COPYRIGHT
> RESTRICTIONS
>
> The copyright law of the United States (Title 17, United States Code) governs the making of photocopies or other reproductions of copyrighted materials.
> Under certain conditions specified in the law, libraries and archives are authorized to furnish a photocopy or other reproduction. One of these specified conditions is that the photocopy or reproduction is not to be "used for any purposes other than private study, scholarship or research." If a user makes a request for, or later uses, a photocopy or reproduction for purposes in excess of "fair use," that user may be liable for copyright infringement.

PRIVACY: An individual depicted in a reproduction has privacy rights as outlined in "Protection of Human Subjects," Title 45 *Code of Federal Regulations*, Pt. 46. The repository reserves the right to require a release from individuals whose privacy may be violated by the publication of an image.

3. All reproductions should include the credit line "Courtesy of the Davidson College Archives."

4. Images may be cropped to suit design and layout, but they may not be altered for drawn upon or manipulated in any way so that they look different from the way they appear in the historical collection.

5. The applicant agrees to send the repository one copy of the work containing the reproduction at no charge.

By signing this application, I accept personnally and on behalf of any organization I represent the conditions set forth above:

Signed:_____   Date:_____

When signed by an authorized agent of the repository, this form constitutes permission for reproduction as outlined in this application.

Signed:_____   Date:_____

WILLIAMS COLLEGE
ARCHIVES AND SPECIAL COLLECTIONS

REQUEST TO PUBLISH

Subject to the following conditions, I/we request permission to publish the following archival or manuscript material from the collections of Williams College Archives and Special Collections (identify below the collection or collections and describe the material precisely):

Bibliographic information of planned publication:

CONDITIONS:

1. Please include the following credit line: Williams College Archives and Special Collections.

2. Permission is granted for one-time use only.

3. Permission to publish fee: When a decision is made to grant publication, please remit a fee of $_____ to Williams College Library, Archives and Special Collections.

4. Williams College does not claim to control the rights of reproduction for materials in its collections. The publishing party assumes all responsibility for clearing reproduction rights and for any infringement of the U.S. Copyright Code.

I/we hereby agree to the conditions specified above.

     Signature: _____

     Name (print): _____

     Date: _____

****

Approved by: _____ Date _____

Williams College

WILLIAMS COLLEGE ARCHIVES AND SPECIAL COLLECTIONS

PERMISSION TO PUBLISH PHOTOGRAPHS

Subject to the following conditions, I/we request permission to reproduce the following photographs from the collections of Williams College Archives and Special Collections:

CONDITIONS:

1. Credit line: Williams College Archives and Special Collections. This credit line must be included for each photograph reproduced.

2. Permission is granted for one-time use only. Photographic material may not be reused without the written permission of the College Archivist.

3. Permission to publish fee: When a decision is made to use a given photograph for publication, please remit a fee of $ _____ per image to Williams College Library, Archives and Special Collections.

4. a) In the case of printed materials, the publisher undertakes to send Williams College Library a copy of the publication containing the photograph(s) listed above. If the work contains no more than two of the Archives' photographs, proofs or tearsheets of the title page and page(s) containing the image(s) and acknowledgement will satisfy this requirement.

   b) In the case of motion picture films, slideshows, and Web sites, the publisher undertakes to send still photographs or photocopies of the title frame/page and the frame/page showing picture credits.

5. Williams College does not claim to control the rights of reproduction for pictorial materials in its collections. The publishing party assumes all responsibility for clearing reproduction rights and for any infringement of the U.S. Copyright Code.

I/we hereby agree to the conditions specified above.

Signature: _____ Date: _____

Name (print): _____ Title: _____

Approved by: _____ Date: _____

LOAN POLICIES AND FORMS

Butler University

4600 Sunset Avenue
Indianapolis, Indiana 46208-3485
OFFICE: (317) 940-9227
FAX: (317) 940-9711

CONDITIONS FOR LOANS
FROM THE BUTLER UNIVERSITY LIBRARIES

1. The borrower recognizes that the material loaned is unique and archival in nature, and will treat it as such.
2. The material will be used only for the purposes of exhibition in the agreed-upon site and for the agreed-upon dates.
3. Materials will be returned immediately upon closure of the exhibition to Special Collections and Rare Books.
4. The borrower agrees to make every reasonable effort to return the materials in the same condition in which they were loaned, and if damage or loss occurs, to pay for repairs or replacements.
5. Loaned materials may not be photocopied, photographed, scanned, traced, or reproduced in any way.
6. Small items will be displayed in cases with no case lights and no direct exposure to sunlight. Preferably cases will have ultra-violet light filtering properties. Items will be displayed on acid-free backing materials. No other materials in the case will touch or rest upon the loaned items. The case will remain locked for the duration of the exhibit.
7. The lender will be acknowledged in exhibition labels with the following credit line: "Courtesy of Butler University Libraries/University Archives."

 **BUTLER UNIVERSITY**

The Butler University Libraries

4600 Sunset Avenue
Indianapolis, Indiana 46208-3485
OFFICE: (317) 940-9227
FAX: (317) 940-9711

Butler University Libraries
Special Collections, Rare Books, and University Archives

Loan Agreement

Butler University Libraries agrees, subject to the conditions printed on the attached sheet, to lend the items below for the purpose of exhibition.

Borrower:_____

Address:_____

Phone:_____

For a period from_____ to_____

Title of exhibition:_____

Location of exhibition:_____

Description of item(s) (including condition and value):_____

_____

_____

_____

_____

_____

_____

The borrower, _____
agrees to observe the conditions on the attached sheet.

Signature:_____

Date:_____

Title:_____

Loan and loan conditions approved for the library by:

Signature:_____

Title:_____

Date:_____

SPECIAL COLLECTIONS, HONNOLD MUDD LIBRARY

TERMS AND CONDITIONS FOR AGREEMENT FOR LOAN

Objects borrowed shall be given special care at all times to insure against loss, damage, and deterioration. The Borrower agrees to meet the special requirements for installation and handling as noted in the *Agreement For Loan* form. The Libraries are to be notified immediately, followed by a full written report including photographs, if damage or loss is discovered. No object may be altered, cleaned, or repaired without the written permission of the Libraries. Objects must be maintained in a building equipped to protect objects from fire, smoke, or flood damage; under 24 hour physical and/or electronic security; and protected from extreme temperatures and humidity, excessive light, and from insects, vermin, dirt, or other environmental hazards. Objects must be handled only by experienced personnel and be secured from damage and theft by appropriate brackets, railings, display cases, or other responsible means.

The Borrower must cover all objects loaned under all-risk, wall-to-wall insurance while en route and on site of exhibition. If the Borrower fails to secure and maintain said insurance, the Borrower will, nevertheless, be required to respond financially in case of loss or damage as if said insurance were in effect.

Packing and transportation shall be by safe methods approved in advanced by the Libraries. Experienced personnel under competent supervision will Unpack and repack the loaned objects. Repacking must be done with the same or similar materials and boxes, and by the same methods as the objects were received. The Libraries will be notified prior to the shipping or the return of the materials. Any additional instructions will be followed.

Government regulations will be adhered to in international shipments. As a rule, the Borrower is responsible for adhering to its country's import/export requirements and the Lender is responsible for adhering to its country's import/export requirements.

Each object shall be labeled and credited to Special Collections.

Agreement to loan the objects does not constitute permission to publish reproductions or photographs of the objects, or any textual content. Such permission must be requested separately in writing and approved in advance. The objects may not be photographed, filmed or televised without advance approval. The Borrower agrees to furnish the Libraries, free of charge, two copies of any catalogs, lists, or other publications relating to the exhibition in which the objects appear or are cited or discussed.

Unless otherwise noted, all packing, transportation, customs, insurance, and other loan-related costs shall be born by the Borrower.

Objects lent must be returned to the Libraries in satisfactory condition by the stated termination date. Any extension of the loan period must be approved in writing by the Special Collections Librarian or her designate and covered by parallel extension of the

SPECIAL COLLECTIONS, HONNOLD/MUDD LIBRARY
AGREEMENT FOR LOAN

<u>Borrower</u>
Name _____

Address _____

_____

Telephone _____ Fax _____

Email _____

<u>Lender</u>
Special Collections, Honnold/Mudd Library
800 North Dartmouth Avenue
Claremont, CA 91711
909-607-3977

In accordance with the terms and conditions on the **Terms and Conditions for Agreement for Loan** form (attached), the items listed below are borrowed for the period:
<u>From:</u>

<u>To:</u>

Shipping and packaging arrangements will be as follows unless otherwise agreed to in writing:

Items to be picked up by

Special requirements for handling, installation, storage, display, etc. (attach continuation sheet if necessary):

Credit Line:

Signature of Lender _____

Title _____

Date _____

Signature of Borrower _____

Title _____

Date _____

insurance coverage. The Libraries reserve the right to recall the object from loan on short notice, if necessary. Furthermore, the Libraries reserve the right to cancel this loan for good cause at any time, and will make every effort to give reasonable notice.

I have read and agree to the above conditions and certify that I am authorized to agree thereto.

Signed: _____

  (Borrower or Authorized Agent)

Title: _____

Date: _____

Approved for the Libraries:
Signed: _____

  (Lender or Authorized Agent)

Title: _____

Date: _____

Williams College

WILLIAMS COLLEGE ARCHIVES AND SPECIAL COLLECTIONS

POLICY ON LOAN FOR EXHIBITION PURPOSES

Material in Williams College Archives and Special Collections is not normally made available for off-campus loan. In the event that an off-campus loan is approved, the following conditions must be met:

1. The organization requesting to borrow material must formally submit a written request, listing each item individually and specifying details of the exhibition, loan period, security and insurance, before the loan will be considered.

2. The borrower agrees to handle and care for the items so that they may be returned to Williams College in the same condition in which they were loaned.

3. The borrower assumes all responsibility and expense for insurance, security, packaging and transportation of the items.

4. Unless otherwise agreed, it is understood that the items are covered door to door by insurance carried by the borrower while in transit and in the borrower's institution or company.

5. In case of loss, breakage or defacement of any item while on loan, the Williams College Librarian must be notified immediately.

6. All items will remain in the possession of the borrower until returned to Williams College.

7. The borrower must give appropriate written credit, both in the exhibition and in any publication deriving from the exhibition, to Williams College Archives and Special Collections.

8. Prior to material leaving Williams College, a copy (photocopy, photograph or microfilm negative) must be made for research and security purposes. This copy will be retained by Williams College and the costs paid by the borrower.

9. All photographic negatives of Williams College originals, either in our possession or out on loan, may not be reproduced without written permission from the College Archivist.

10. Publication of any photographs or illustrations reproduced from Williams College Archives and Special Collections must adhere to previously adopted policies regarding publication fees, unless otherwise agreed.

11. Items may not be photographically reproduced without express and written permission from a representative of Williams College Archives and Special Collections.

12. Williams College reserves the right to recall any or all of the items on seven days written notice.

13. The borrower must agree to any additional stipulations of loan as detailed on attached pages.

Williams College

WILLIAMS COLLEGE ARCHIVES AND SPECIAL COLLECTIONS

LOAN CONTRACT

The following items are on loan to _____ from

Williams College Archives and Special Collections for _____

purposes only, subject to the conditions stated on the attached page.

Duration of loan: _____

Item(s):

Accession/Call No.   Material/Collection

WILLIAMS COLLEGE ARCHIVES AND SPECIAL COLLECTIONS

LOAN CONTRACT CONDITIONS

1. The borrower agrees to handle and care for these items so that they may be returned to Williams College Archives and Special Collections in the same condition in which they were loaned.

2. In case of loss, breakage, or defacement of any of these items while on loan, please notify the Williams College Librarian immediately.

3. All items will remain in the possession of the borrower until returned to Williams College Archives.

4. The borrower agrees to give appropriate written credit, in any exhibition or publication, to Williams College Archives and Special Collections.

5. The borrower agrees to any additional stipulations of loan as detailed on attached pages.

Signature: _____

    Date: _____

Name (printed): _____

Institution/Department: _____

****

Loan authorized by: _____

    Date: _____

ORAL HISTORY PERMISSION FORMS

Davidson College Archives
Oral History Collection

The purpose of the Davidson College Archives Oral History Collection is to gather and preserve interviews for historical and scholarly use. A tape recording of your interview will be made the by the interviewer and any transcription thereof which may be made will be added to the Davidson College Archives. These materials will be made available for research by scholars, for scholarly publications, and other related purposes, unless restricted by you.

- - - - - - - - -

I, _____ , have read the above and, in view of the scholarly
(Interviewee, please print)

value of this interview, I knowingly and voluntarily permit the Davidson College Archives the full use of this interview. I hereby assign all my rights of every kind whatever, including copyright, pertaining to this interview and any subsequent interviews in this series, both during my lifetime and after my death, whether or not such rights are now known, to the Davidson College Archives.

_____
Interviewee (signature)

_____
Date

WILLIAMS COLLEGE ARCHIVES AND SPECIAL COLLECTIONS

EXPLANATION OF LEGAL AGREEMENT

The enclosed Legal Agreement is designed to enable you, the interviewee, to determine the terms of access to and to the use of the oral history interview in which you participated. The options which we have set forth are for your convenience and should not be regarded as exclusive. You may add others as you see fit, or you may change the wording to suit your purposes.

1. Access and Restrictions

Although there may be no need to limit access to the interview (especially if it relates to activities occurring several years in the past), the option of placing restrictions on access to the taped interview, and any transcript which may be made from it, is always available to the interviewee.

2. Publication and Quotation: Literary Property Rights

We are offering two alternatives with respect to literary property rights to material in the oral history interviews:
A. The literary property rights may be assigned immediately to the College; or,
B. The literary property rights may be retained by the interviewee until such time as he/she deems it appropriate to assign them to Williams College.

In the latter case, no one may publish the interview in whole or in part, nor may anyone quote from it without explicit permission from the interviewee. Interviewees who choose to retain literary property rights may permit brief quotations without explicit written permission in each case so as to avoid being bothered by numerous requests from researchers.

When literary property rights are assigned to Williams College, permission of the interviewee to quote from or to publish excerpts from the interview is not required. In this case, it is the policy of the Williams College Archives to permit brief quotations essential to a complete work but not to permit publication of the entire interview.

(Retention of literary property rights does not, by itself, affect access to interviews, nor does it prohibit researchers from paraphrasing or citing interviews as the sources of ideas.)

3. Copying and Dissemination

In the absence of interviewee restrictions to the contrary it is the practice of the Williams College Archives to provide copies of open oral history interviews to any researcher upon request.

WILLIAMS COLLEGE ARCHIVES AND SPECIAL COLLECTIONS

LEGAL AGREEMENT

I,_____, do hereby give to Williams College, for use and administration therein, all my rights, title and interest, except as hereinafter provided, to the tape recording, and any transcripts which may be made from it, of the interview conducted as part of the Williams College Oral History Project. The gift of this material is made subject to the following terms and conditions.

1. Access and Restrictions

Please check the statement(s) reflecting your wishes with respect to access to your interview.

____ I wish to make the interview available on an unrestricted basis to anyone applying to use the resources of the Williams College Archives.

____ Researchers must first obtain my permission in writing to have access to the interview.

____ I wish to restrict the use of the interview for a specified period of time. (Please indicate which of the options below are in accordance with your wishes.)

     I desire that my interview be:
        ____ closed for a period of _____ years.
        ____ closed until my death.
        ____ closed until my death and for a period of _____ years thereafter.

2. Publication and Quotation: Literary Property Rights

Please check the statement(s) reflecting your wishes with respect to literary property rights.

____ I do not choose to retain literary property rights to the interview, and I wish to assign them immediately to Williams College.

___ I wish to retain literary property rights to the interview for a period of _____ years, or until my death, whichever is the later, at which time the literary property rights shall be assigned to Williams College.

3. Copying and Dissemination

Please check the statement(s) reflecting your wishes with respect to dissemination of the interview.

___ Copies of the interview may be provided upon request to any researcher.

___ Copying of the interview or portions thereof, except as needed to maintain an adequate number of research copies available in the Williams College Library, is expressly prohibited, and copies may not be disseminated outside the Library.

___ The limitation (if any) to copying and dissemination shall be in effect until _____, at which time current Archives practice shall prevail.

Signed _____

Date _____

Accepted _____

Date _____

Appendix

Appendix: Responses to Question 19

Adams State College, Nielsen Library, Alamosa, Colorado – Research archive of Ruth Marie Colville, a local historian; arrowhead/artifact collection; materials about San Luis Valley/Colorado/New Mexico history

Albion College, Stockwell-Mudd Libraries, Albion, Michigan – MacGregor Plan Americana; Marvin Vann '40 Collection; Marie Guy Kimball Poetry Collection; J. Harlan Bretz Collection

Alfred University, Herrick Memorial Library, Alfred, New York – Howells/Frechette Collection; Openhym Collection of Modern British Literature & Social History

Augustana College, Thomas Tredway Library, Rock Island, Illinois – Charles XV collection, which contains many books about the French Revolution in French, gifted to the College in 1862 by Charles XV, King of Sweden

Augustana College, Mikkelsen Library, Sioux Falls, South Dakota – Collection of Scandinavian (primarily Norwegian) immigrant literature

Austin College, Abell Library, Sherman, Texas – Julio Berzunza Collection on Alexander the Great

Barton College, Hackney Library, Wilson, North Carolina – Examples of fine binding, approximately 30 books with fore-edge paintings listed in catalog

Bellarmine College, Brown Library, Louisville, Kentucky – Thomas Merton Archives.

Bowdoin College, Library, Brunswick, Maine – Pre-1601 Manuscripts, 17th Century Manuscripts, African-American History Resources, Political History Resources, Civil War Resources, Joshua Lawrence Chamberlain Resources

Bucknell University, Bertrand Library, Lewisburg, Pennsylvania – Several small collections of Anglo-Irish literary figures; significant collection of George Bernard Shaw manuscript materials; collection of manuscript materials of Oliver St. John Gogarty; two Civil War manuscript collections; Anna Slifer-Walls Papers and the Linn Family Papers.

Butler University, Butler University Libraries, Indianpolis, Indiana – Charters Collection of South Seas materials; Eliza Blaker Collection; Gaar Williams-Kin Hubbard Collection; Lincoln Collection; Harold E. Johnson Sibelius collection; Dellinger Education Collection; Etheridge Knight collection

Canisius College, Bouwhuis Library, Buffalo, New York – Four books of hours listed in Di Ricci Census and the Koburger Bible; Centenary College – Autograph Collection; Genealogy Collection; Centenary Archives; Picture Collection

The Claremont Colleges, The Libraries of the Claremont Colleges, Claremont, California – Clary Oxford Collection; Bodman Renaissance Collection; Philbrick Collection of Dramatic Arts and Theatre History; Mason and Wagner Collections of Western Americana; Hoover Collection of Mining and Metallurgy; Water Resources Collection; McPherson Collection by and about Women; Ellen Browning Scripps Collection; Woodford Collection of Geology; Archives of the Claremont Colleges

Coe College, Stewart Memorial Library, Cedar Rapids, Iowa – William Shirer papers

Colorado College, Tutt Library, Colorado Springs, Colorado – Helen Hunt Jackson Papers

Culver-Stockton College, Carl Johann Memorial Library, Canton, Missouri – Aubrey Allen's Pencil Collection; Christian Church (Disciples of Christ) history; Culver-Stockton College History

Davidson College, E.H. Little Library, Davidson, North Carolina – William P. Cummings Map Collection; Bruce Rogers Collection; Thomas Wolfe Collection; Golden Cockerel Press

Earlham College, Earlham College Libraries, Richmond, Indiana – Friends United Meeting Archives; D. Elton Trueblood Papers; Cassell Rare Book Collection

Eastern New Mexico University, Golden Library, Portales, New Mexico – Jack Williamson Science Fiction Library; New Mexico history; University archives

Eastern Washington University, JFK Library, Cheney, Washington – Edward S. Curtis, *The North American Indian*; Washington Water Power Co. Records; Spokane Community Action **King Cole Papers; Ninety-Nine NW Section Records** Council Records;

Elmira College, Gannett-Tripp Library, Elmira, New York – Mark Twain – first editions, photographs, letters, manuscripts; Archive of the New York State Federation of Women's Clubs; Charles Tomlinson Griffes Collection

Evergreen State College, Evergreen State College Library, Olympia, Washington – Evergreen State College Archives; Nisqually Delta Association Archives; Chicano Archives

Fitchburg State College, Amelia V. Gallucci-Cirio Library, Fitchburg, Massachusetts - Robert Cormier Collection; Robert Salvatore Collection

Francis Marion University, James A. Rogers Library, Florence, South Carolina – George A. Henty Children's book collection; Thomas G. Samworth Hunting and Sporting Collection; James A. Rogers Collection; University Archives; Books about Francis Marion

Gannon University, Nash Library, Erie, Pennsylvania – John G. Carney Erie History Collection; Rev. Charles Costello ERIE Diocese Collection; Archbishop John Hark Gannon Collection

Goshen College, Harold and Wilma Good Library, Goshen Indiana – The Mennonite Historical Library is the most comprehensive collection of printed materials by and about Mennonites and related Anabaptist groups (e.g. Amish and Hutterites) in the world. The college library owns the Hartzler Music Collection, a significant collection of 19th-century American tunebooks and hymnals.

Goucher College, Julia Rogers Library, Baltimore, Maryland - Jane Austen Collection; Sara Haardt & H.L. Mencken, Brownlee Sands Corrin Collection, Winslow Collection of Political Memorabilia; Passano Collection of Women of the South during the Civil War

Hamilton College, Daniel Burke Library, Hamilton, New York – Beinecke Lesser Antilles Collection; Ezra Pound Collection; Communal Societies Collection (with an emphasis on the Shakers)

Hanover College, Agnes Brown Duggan Library, Hanover, Indiana –reference works and collections dealing with Indiana and local history, Hanover College and the Presbyterian Church in Indiana; rare first editions; works about Western Exploration; works by prominent Indiana authors.

Harding University, Brackett Library, Searcy, Arkansas – Williams-Miles History of Chemical Education Collection

Humboldt State University, Library, Arcata, California – collections on the natural resources, Native peoples, and primary industries of Northwestern California, including the history of Humboldt State University

Illinois College, Schewe Library, Jacksonville, Illinois – Lincolniana; Civil War Collection

Indiana University South Bend, Franklin D. Schurz Library, South Bend, Indiana – Casaday Theatre Collection; Christianson Lincoln Collection

Iowa Wesleyan College, Chadwick Library, Mt. Pleasant, Iowa – Zwingli F Meyer Collection of German-American Methodism; C.S. Rogers Collection of Henry County newspapers; Earl Newsom Collection of John Edward Newsom and Emma Day Newsom letters and papers (1876-1930's)

Jamestown College, Raugust Library, Jamestown, North Dakota – Stroth Collection – Nazi childrens materials; Scottish Collection

Lafayette College, David Bishop Skillman Library, Easton, Pennsylvania – Incunabula, including a copy of the Nuremburg Chronicle, examples of fine printing from the past 200 years, the Marquis de Lafayette Collection, Stephen Crane Collection, and the Jane Conneen Miniature Book Collection.

Lipscomb College, Beaman Library, Nashville, Tennessee –Ernest R. Bailey Hymnology Collection

Manhattanville College, Library, Purchase, New York– finding aids at www.manhattanville.edu/library/specialcollections/index.htm

Massachusetts College of Liberal Arts, Freel Library, North Adams, Massachusetts – Randy Trabold Photograph Collection; Local History Collection; College Archives

Methodist College, Davis Library, Fayetteville, North Carolina – Lafayette Collection: letters by and about, books and memorabilia about the Marquis de Lafayette

Mills College, F.W. Olin Library, Oakland, California – Darias Milhaud Collection; Parton Collection (rare books on dance); Fine and private press books collection; Albert Bender Papers

Mississippi College, Leland Speed Library, Clinton, Mississippi – Osborn Collection (20th century American history and presidential studies)

Moravian College, Reeves Library, Bethlehem, Pennsylvania – Moravian Church history; Female Seminary Library Collection; Men's Theological Seminary Library Collection

Mount St. Mary's College & Seminary, Library, Emmitsburg, Maryland – Catholicism in Early America; Marylandia

Mount Union College, Library, Alliance, Ohio – stamp collection with extensive worldwide coverage

Muhlenberg College, Trexler Library, Allentown, Pennsylvania – Brennen Map Collection; Abram Samuels Sheet Music Collection; Paul McHale Congressional Papers

North Central College, Library, Napeville, Illinois– College Archives; Harris W. Fawell Congressional Papers; Suburban Studies Archives

Northern Michigan University, Lydia M. Olson Library, Marquette, Michigan – Moses Coit Tyler Collection; John Voelker Papers; Dominic Jacobetti Papers; Cleveland-Cliffs, Inc. Papers

Northern State University, Williams Library, Aberdeen, South Dakota – Harriet Montgomery Water Resource Collection – large collection of papers and documents relating to the upper Missouri River Watershed; Ben Smelty Rare Mathematics Book Collection

Oberlin College, Library, Oberlin, Ohio – Oberliniana; Jack Schaefer Collection; History of the Book Collection; Anti-slavery Collection; Goodkind collection; Spanish Drama Collection; Spanish Historical Novel Collection; Seal Press Collection; Natural History Collection; Travel and Exploration Collection; Dime Novels Collection; Socialist Pamphlets Collection; WWII Propaganda Collection; War of 1812 Collection; Edwin Arlington Robinson Collection

Ohio Wesleyan University, Libraries, Delaware, Ohio – William D. Bayley Walt Whitman Collection, guide; Brwoning collection; Spanish Civil war Collection; Greenaway collection; Gunsankes collection (art, artifacts, books); Methodist Historical collection; OWU Archives

Otterbein College, Courtright Memorial Library, Westerville, Ohio – Lucinda Lenore Merriss Cornell Diaries Collection

Our Lady of the Lake University, Sueltenfuss Library, San Antonio, Texas – 15th Century French illuminated Book of Hours; early pastorelas (Spanish Folk Plays); 1st edition of Our Catholic Heritage in Texas

Plattsburg State College, Feinburg Library, Plattsburg, New York – Rockwell Kent Collection

Queens College, Everett Library, Charlotte, North Carolina – The Queens College Collection, The Local History Collection, and the Art of the Book-Maker.

Randolph-Macon College, McGraw-Page Library, Ashland, Virginia – Archive of the Virginia Conference of the United Methodist Church; J. Rives Childs Collection; Henry Miller Collection; Casanova Collection

Reed College, Library, Portland, Oregon – Lloyd J. Reynolds Collection (calligraphy, design); Antiquarian Map Collection; Belgian collection; Janet Walker-Binford Collection (travel, children's books, publishing); A.E. Doyle Collection (architecture); Artists Books Collection

Rollins College, Olin Library, Winter Park, Florida – William Sloane Kennedy Collection of Whitmaniana; Marjorie Kinnan Rawlings Collection; A. Reynolds Morse Collection of M.P. Shiel; Henry Nehrling Collection of horticulture; Jessie B. Rittenhouse Collection of 20th Century Poetry; Florida Collection

St. John Fisher College, Lavery Library, Rochester, New York – George P. Decker Papers; Frederick Douglass Collection

Salisbury University, Blackwell Library, Salisbury, Maryland – Leslie P. Dryden Collection (genealogical collection)

Siena College, Standish Library, Loudonville, New York – Treasurers from the J. Spencer & Patricia Standish Library's Convivum Collection

Simpson College, Start-Kilgour Memorial Library, Redding, California – Sears Lehmann Collection of Ancient Pottery

Smith College, Libraries, Northampton, Massachusetts – Collections of Incunabula; the Papers of Sylvia Plath, Virginia Woolf, and others; holdings in English and American literature, botany, history of science, economics, early children's literature, seventeenth- and eighteenth-century English drama and political pamphlets, early lithographic books, British phonology and lexicography, and nineteenth-century American trade cards; Sophia Smith Collection.

Sweet Briar College, Libraries, Sweet Briar, Virginia – W.H. Auden; T.E. Lawrence; George Meredith, Evelyn Day Mullen; Virginia Woolf; Fanny B. Fletcher Archives (repository for the records of the College in addition to scrapbooks, photographs, and diaries

Texas Tech University, Libraries, Lubbock, Texas – Rare and early printed books and maps, limited editions and fine bindings. With a primary focus of 19th- and 20thcentury American and British literature, its in-print collection of Joseph Conrad is perhaps the strongest in the world. Other author collections include: W.H. Auden, John Donne, Rudyard Kipling, Walt Whitman, Marianne Moore, Kay Boyle, and James Dickey. Other Collections include: Southwest Collection, Oriental Collection, Archive of the Vietnam Conflict.

University of Illinois-Springfield, Brookens Library, Springfield, Illinois – IRAD; Oral History Collection; Handy Colony Collection

University of North Carolina-Pembroke, Sampson-Livermore Library, Pembroke, North Carolina – US Representative Charlie Rose's Congressional Papers; Fuller/Rhodes Family Papers

University of South Carolina-Aiken, Library, Aiken, South Carolina – Gregg-Graniteville Archives

University of Texas-Brownsville, Arnulfo L. Oliveira, Brownsville, Texas – Menton Murray Papers; Collections on the Mexican-American War and the Palo Alto National Battlefield

University of Toledo, Carlson Library, Toledo, Ohio - Bibles in different languages

Urbana University, Swedenborg Memorial Library, Urbana, Ohio – Swedenborg Collection with items dating from the eighteenth century, and the Swedenborgian Collections of books and other items by and about the Church of the New Jerusalem.

Wabash College, Lilly Library, Crawfordsville, Indiana – The Edmund O. and Mary Hovey Manuscript Collection; Dewitt O'Kieffe Collection of Early Western Americana; Dave Gerard Cartoon Collection; Ted Steeg Productions Archive

Wagner College, Horrmann Library, State Island, New York – Edwin Markham, local poet, 1852-1940

Walla Walla College, Peterson Memorial Library, College Place, Washington – Pacific Northwest Seventh Day Adventist collections

Wellesley College, Margaret Clapp Library, Wellesley, Massachusetts – English Poetry Collection; Plimpton Collection of Italian Literature from the 14th to 17th centuries; Elbert Collection of materials on slavery, emancipation, and Reconstruction;

West Liberty State College, Paul N. Elbin Library, West Liberty, West Virginia – Nelle R. Krise rare Book Room; West liberty State College Archives; College Museum; Henry Lash Sheet Music Collection

West Virginia Wesleyan College, Annie Merner Pfieffer Library, Buckhannon, West Virginia – Jones Lincoln Collection; Pearl Buck manuscripts

Western Carolina University, Hunter Library, Cullowhee, North Carolina – Horace Kephart collection; Cherokee documents in foreign archives collection

Wheaton College, Buswell Memorial Library, Wheaton, Illinois – Papers of Jonathan Blanchard (noted abolitionist), Madeleine L'Engle, Frederick Buechner, Malcolm Muggeridge, Jacques Ellul (Sociologist/Ethicist), Margaret Landon, Kenneth Landon (State Dept. official), Honorable Daniel R. Coats (Senator/Ambassador). Rare book holdings provide substantial coverage on English Literature, particularly Johnson and Boswell; Southeast Asia; and Bible texts.

Whitman College, Penrose Library, Walla Walla, Washington – Materials relating to the pacific Northwest; ABCFM Activities; Skokomish Indian materials compiled by Myron Fells; Local business and social records; Professional papers of D.C. Graham (Chinese materials)